Be CentsAble

CHRISSY PATE is a former high school teacher and mother of two. Once she became a stay-at-home mom, Chrissy learned how to replace the money she used to earn by saving money for her family. She took her newfound money-saving skills—along with her love of teaching and turned it into a way of helping others save money by creating BeCentsable, the company she cofounded with Kristin McKee. Chrissy lives with her family near Kansas City, Missouri.

KRISTIN MCKEE currently lives in Phoenix, Arizona, with her amazing family (husband, Danny, and two perfectly wonderful children). She worked as a financial analyst for several years before being lucky enough to become a stay-at-home mom. Now, between being Mommy and wife, blogging, and comanaging BeCentsable, she dreams of being a teacher and chef.

Be CentsAble

HOW TO CUT YOUR
HOUSEHOLD BUDGET
IN HALF

Chrissy Pate and Kristin McKee

A PLUME BOOK

PLUME
Published by the Penguin Group
Penguin Group (USA) Inc., 375 Hudson Street, New York, New York 10014, U.S.A.
Penguin Group (Canada), 90 Eglinton Avenue East, Suite 700, Toronto, Ontario, Canada
M4P 2Y3 (a division of Pearson Penguin Canada Inc.)
Penguin Books Ltd., 80 Strand, London WC2R 0RL, England
Penguin Ireland, 25 St. Stephen's Green, Dublin 2, Ireland (a division of Penguin Books Ltd.)
Penguin Group (Australia), 250 Camberwell Road, Camberwell, Victoria 3124, Australia
(a division of Pearson Australia Group Pty. Ltd.)
Penguin Books India Pvt. Ltd., 11 Community Centre, Panchsheel Park,
New Delhi – 110 017, India
Penguin Group (NZ), 67 Apollo Drive, Rosedale, North Shore 0632, New Zealand
(a division of Pearson New Zealand Ltd.)
Penguin Books (South Africa) (Pty.) Ltd., 24 Sturdee Avenue, Rosebank,
Johannesburg 2196, South Africa

Penguin Books Ltd., Registered Offices: 80 Strand, London WC2R 0RL, England

First published by Plume, a member of Penguin Group (USA) Inc.

First Printing, April 2010
10 9 8 7 6 5 4 3 2 1

Copyright © Christina Pate and Kristin McKee, 2010
All rights reserved

℗ REGISTERED TRADEMARK—MARCA REGISTRADA

LIBRARY OF CONGRESS CATALOGING-IN-PUBLICATION DATA

Pate, Chrissy.
Be CentsAble : how to cut your household budget in half / Chrissy Pate and Kristin McKee.
p. cm.
Includes index.
ISBN 978-0-452-29624-4 (pbk. : alk. paper)   1. Consumer education.   2. Home
economics—Accounting.   I. McKee, Kristin.   II. Title.
TX335.P362 2010
332.024—dc22
2009046240

Printed in the United States of America
Set in Dante and Montag • Designed by Chris Welch

FROM CHRISSY PATE

To my husband, Chris, who has always loved and
supported me in all I do, and my girls, April and Ava,
who are my everything

FROM KRISTIN MCKEE

To Chrissy, for understanding me and my craziness
(and liking me anyway)
To Danny, my rock, without you I'd have nothing
To my kids, for your infectious happiness and love,
you keep me going

Contents

Acknowledgments

We have been blessed to have so many wonderful people help us in our journey. Though we can't thank everyone by name we must thank Anna Bannister, Janet O'Connor, Melissa Banks, and Michele Wilt for all their hard work and dedication.

To our wonderful editor, Meghan Stevenson, and our agent, Victora Horn, who helped encourage and support us in writing this book.

We are especially grateful to Dion Lim, who did our first local news story, and Elisabeth Leamy, for our first national news piece. Special thanks to Laura Thornquist and Rob Yagmin for all their help with press.

To all the great money-saving blogs that inspire and motivate us to save money, and all of our BeCentsable educators for helping BeCentsable grow across the country.

And finally, to all of our family and friends who helped and supported us when we felt like we couldn't go on!

Introduction

Have you ever learned a new skill or bit of information that, once put into action, seemed so simple and easy you wondered how you had lived so long without knowing it? Well, we have! We've learned to use simple strategies to significantly cut our household budget. We can teach you how to do it, too—without cutting out the brands you like, without cutting back significantly on the things you typically buy, and without spending hours each week clipping coupons and scrimping on every little thing you do. We can teach you how to be "centsable" *and* sane so you can keep more of your hard-earned money in your pocket.

We are wives and mothers managing two very typical families. Just a few years ago, we found ourselves putting more money out than we were bringing in. Even after diligently cutting back on all other budget categories (like cable, Internet, cell phones, insurance, subscriptions, and memberships) we were still overspending, specifically on those things we bought for our household consumption (food, health and beauty aids, and baby care and pet products).

Until we began to actively address this area of our spending, we assumed the price on the shelf was the price we had to pay. Now, though, we have cut our personal spending on the same items in half! How did we do this? By tackling our own budgeting issues with hours of research and experimentation, until we found a system that allowed us to make dramatic cuts in the amount of money we spend on household items without changing the way we live our lives. Our success had such a great impact on our lives we couldn't help but share it with everyone we knew. Together we created an easy, centsable program that will teach you to cut your household budget in half without drastically altering your lifestyle.

Chrissy's Story

Chrissy, a thirty-three-year-old stay-at-home mom, was born and raised in Missouri. Before they had kids, she and her husband, Chris, a high school physical education teacher and coach, were very comfortable financially. They had little debt, no car payments, and a great start on their retirement. But then the expensive part of life came along.

After the birth of their first child, Chrissy left her job as a high school special education teacher to stay home. A short six months later, they were expecting baby number two and had no time to think about how much they were spending.

Shortly after the birth of their second child, Chris and Chrissy took a Dave Ramsey class together. The class taught them how to gain control over their budget and encouraged them to set high financial goals. They had dreams of traveling around the world with their girls and buying a retirement home in Hawaii. They wanted to be able to pay for their children's college education. Both Chris and Chrissy realized they needed to change their budget today to have the future they dreamed of, and they set a high goal for themselves: they would put extra money aside every month to pay their house off in about five years then use what they had been spending on their mortgage to save for college and retirement.

They found several areas of their budget that could be cut back or eliminated but it wasn't quite enough. They still needed an extra $250 a month to help reach their goals. It was Chris who came up with the solution. They could cut their household budget. They were spending about $800 a month on their groceries, personal care items, cleaning supplies, baby needs, and pet food. Even though they had already dismissed this idea once, Chris challenged Chrissy to cut back to $500 a month. Chrissy was convinced that $800 was a fixed cost. It was just how much it cost to feed their family. Now, however skeptical, she agreed to try.

Chrissy had always considered herself a smart shopper. She purchased items in bulk, bought mostly generic products from the local grocery store and very little processed food, and would often cook from scratch not only for the health benefits but because she enjoyed it.

She began by only buying items on sale, adding more generics to her cart (experimenting with less expensive diapers and paper products), and even cutting out some things altogether. After two months with little success, she was disappointed, to say the least. She felt like her family was sacrificing a lot for not a lot of benefit. She even considered taking a small part-time job to make some extra money. But with two little ones at home, she knew this was unrealistic. She decided there had to be a way to make the $500 budget work. She also knew that she had to make it into a fun challenge, otherwise everyone would be miserable.

Chrissy began researching online by reading a couple of blogs she found. It was true: there were shoppers saving loads of money each week and still buying brand-name foods (lots of it!); to her surprise they were doing it with coupons. But she was doubtful; she couldn't believe coupons would work for her. She barely had time to take a shower—how would she find time to sit down and clip, sort, and file coupons every week, read the circulars, plan a menu and a shopping list, and actually get to the store? Then she discovered strategies that seemed a perfect fit for her time limitations. Once she started to implement some of these coupon strategies, she started to save real money and was hooked. She was excited about her discoveries and was eager to learn more and share what she'd discovered.

Kristin's Story

Like Chrissy, Kristin was raised in Missouri, where she met her husband, Danny, and started their family. Marrying young, Kristin and Danny worked through many years of financial insecurity before their own "centsabilities" kicked in. To be fair we should say *her* centsabilities. Kristin's husband had always been financially responsible; she was on the learning curve.

During the early years of their marriage, they always managed to pay their bills, though they often lived paycheck to paycheck. Their first Christmas together they put all their gift purchases— about $2,000 worth—on a Visa card. It took them four years to pay that Christmas off. A long and hard but valuable lesson!

They both worked full-time while attending college, but they still accumulated about $30,000 each in student loans. Danny completed college first and went to work in the avionics field, then a few years later Kristin completed a degree in economics and started her career as a financial analyst. The interesting thing about being a financial analyst is that it doesn't affect one's personal financial life. Certainly she was able to analyze financial matters and situations for her clients, but she couldn't separate herself from her own finances enough to analyze them effectively!

Kristin and Danny's financial transformation occurred in baby steps. In 2001, they purchased a home. Just three years after buying their home and graduating from college, they discovered that they were expecting their first child. They began doing all the things expectant parents do—redecorating rooms and buying furniture, gadgets, clothes, cute little toys and cuddly things . . . and diapers. They were amazed at the cost of having a child, but without a good example of reasonable "new baby" spending, they were putting more pressure on their already stressed budget. More than ever they felt they *needed* two incomes, so after Kristin's maternity leave, she went back to work full-time. They discovered what many new parents come to realize. Just the cost of diapers, wipes, formula, clothing, and child care was eating up nearly all their second income. As if they had no choice, they continued shopping the same way, spending an hour or two wandering around the store grabbing whatever things caught their eye. They still had little savings, a small amount of credit card debt, a car payment, and those pesky student loans.

Six months before the birth of their second child, Kristin was offered a voluntary layoff with severance. She decided to venture into scary, uncharted (but much desired and appreciated) territory—a single-income family with children. At least, Kristin thought, she would finally be able to really focus on things at home. But being a stay-at-home parent comes with its own challenges and learning curve. Soon, her attempts to be organized and in control were tossed out the window and weekly shopping became yet another thing she had to squeeze in and rush through. Kristin, Danny, and the kids always went to the store on the weekends as a family and wandered around until the kids got antsy, tired, or hungry. They rarely attempted to use coupons—most of Kristin's coupons were sitting in a pile on the counter unclipped, unsorted, and usually expired. They seldom had a defined list, just a rough idea of what they needed and a lot of impulses. It became clear that continuing these habits would not work for their family's long-term financial health. Kristin's severance would be ending soon and they would officially have just one income.

Kristin did have one bit of good sense . . . in order to save money, find fun and inexpensive activities for her and the kids, and avoid feeling trapped at home, she joined a local mothers' support group in her town. It was through this group that Kristin met Chrissy and they became good friends. Their two oldest children were in the same playgroup and they attended the same church. They quickly found common ground in their family's similarities.

When Initiative and Good Timing Collide

Even though we had very different upbringings, and undeniably different approaches to finances, we learned that fundamentally we had the same goals:

1. We wanted to be home with our children.
2. We wanted to make smarter decisions with our money.
3. We wanted to do these two things as simply as possible.

Together, we discussed how our families could live without debt and pinpointed our greatest budget challenges. Not surprisingly, our household expenses were the biggest culprits. With two kids in diapers, a husband, and two large dogs, our household goods, toiletries, and groceries each month cost almost the same amount as our mortgages! Even more surprising was what we discovered when we started looking for ways to cut back.

We'd heard of frugal shoppers spending mere pennies on a meal for their entire family, saving that extra money to pay for everything from a house and new car to college. Of course, we were skeptical. We did not want to dramatically change our lifestyle or sacrifice the things our families liked. We refused to reuse foil and plastic wrap or save little scraps of food for use in an obscure weekend goulash. We have small children, very busy lives, and we treasure the convenience of many of the things self-proclaimed frugal zealots scoff at.

At first we didn't even know where to begin. Despite desperate searching, we found nothing that really helped us. Most of the resources we came across left something out. We checked out dozens of books at the library, most of them suggesting changes we knew wouldn't work for our families in the long term, like buying *only* generics and cutting out everything enjoyable and fun! Others stopped short of presenting a total solution, focusing only on using coupons or only on cooking from scratch. We wanted something all-encompassing, a total solution to household savings.

We turned to the only truly useful resources we could find: blogs. After reading through dozens upon dozens of websites and forums, we were amazed to learn that not only did we know nothing about the proper ways to save money on household goods, but there were families of four, six, and even eight shopping for less than *half* of what we were spending, and they were still buying brand-name products—even organics! After countless hours, and too many websites to remember or list, we decided we ought to try some of the savings techniques for ourselves.

In the fall of 2007, we began our shopping experiment. We would research a new "strategy" and then head to the store each week to try it out. One bit of information would lead to another and soon we were tangled in a virtual spiderweb of frugality advice. Weeding through poorly explained or clearly unethical information to find the tips and tricks we could use in the long term was exhausting. We realized that this was a larger undertaking than we had imagined.

Our perseverance eventually paid off. Having the knowledge and resources to find deep savings is inspiring in itself, but true satisfaction comes from actually achieving those savings. When we finally saw our efforts cutting a significant 20%–25% from our grocery bills each week, coupons became as valuable to us as cash. Learning where we could get double the value for a coupon (i.e., "double coupons") and then learning to time our coupon use around store sales was exhilarating! We continued to add to our savings opportunities by researching and trying new strategies, such as "stacking" (using more than one strategy to buy a single item), and understanding how to make the most of store incentive programs and promotions.

Practice Makes Perfect

We became even more driven (and inspired) once we experienced the unbelievable feat of getting items for free. If you don't believe it, we don't blame you—we didn't either, at first. On occasion, you can get items your family will use anyway for free. With meticulous planning and timing, we were once able to get tons of batteries for free and earn store credit toward our next purchase: Not long after reading about how to stack savings strategies to buy a single item at a deep discount, we noted a great sale on batteries in our weekly circular. We also saw that the store was promoting them through an incentive program—we could earn in-store credit just for buying these batteries that we needed and that were on sale. Deciding this was the perfect opportunity to test our new knowledge, we found a store coupon and a coupon from the manufacturer of the batteries and went shopping. We were so amazed when we were both holding our $15 store credit just a few minutes later that we nearly ran out of the store . . . partly from our excitement and partly out of fear the store employees might decide we'd done something wrong.

We were so proud of ourselves after each shopping trip that we would rush home to show our husbands our loot. We suppose it's the nature of men that led our husbands to be competitive about our savings. We'd put all of our items out on display and ask them to guess what we'd spent—not what the items cost but what we had put out in cash for them. Our husbands would guess and always be appropriately surprised and proud of our savings before inquiring . . . "So, what did Chrissy spend?" "What did Kristin spend?" And of course, "Why did she spend less than you?!"

Although amusing, this brings up an important point that we reiterate to everyone in our programs. It's the underlying premise of *Be CentsAble*: *we will not tell you what your budget should or could be.* We want to help you do the most you can for your family . . . nothing more, nothing less. You can only compare *what you come to spend* with *what you used to spend.* You can't compare yourself with any other family and be discouraged because you aren't meeting their low weekly budget. Conversely, you can't assume you are doing the best you can because your budget is lower than another family's. Each family has different needs and different preferences. Each family is willing to make changes in areas that help in different ways.

Our families are a great example of how needs vary widely from household to household. Chrissy's family puts great importance on eating healthy, and they are willing to pay a premium for organics. Aside from that, her family has no specific dietary needs or restrictions. Kristin's family also puts an emphasis on healthy, organic foods but must do so under more restrictive dietary concerns, which requires added expense. Chrissy's husband must take lunch to work with him each day, whereas Kristin's husband comes home for lunch. These small differences account for variations in our budgets. When Kristin relocated to Arizona, we discovered geographic location can make a big difference in a weekly grocery budget. In the Midwest, grains are much less expensive than they are in the Southwest. On the flip side, produce is much cheaper in the Southwest. The bottom line is that we would waste a lot of time trying to "outsave" each other rather than just achieving the lowest budget our families' lifestyles will support.

Our families' needs mean that we don't always get the lowest possible price. Sometimes we pay a little more for a brand or type of food we want or need. This prompted us to find ways to save that don't involve coupons. We are able to save money even on those pricier specialty items for our family because we've researched the best ways to do it. For example, we both like to bake our own bread. We felt it was healthier and wanted to make it a money-saving effort as well. We quickly saw that whole wheat flour and yeast can be quite expensive, and that finding coupons for these items is unlikely. We work around this, however, by buying as much as we can use during the sales cycles for these products, or by buying them in bulk from a local natural foods store. Doing this saves us 40%–60%!

Some of the strategies we teach have little to do with actual shopping but are just as important and useful. One *aha!* moment came for us when we learned a better way to plan our meals. We discovered it worked best to look at the weekly ads and our pantry first, and then make a menu for the week. Of course it sounds like a no-brainer now, but many people do it in the reverse order. This simple change had a huge impact on the money we spent, the number of things we had to buy at the store, and the time it took us to get it accomplished.

After several months spent learning and practicing these strategies, and countless mistakes along the way, we realized we were cutting our expenses in measurable ways. One evening, Chrissy analyzed her spending and saw she was now spending under $350 on household items. Likewise, Kristin's family had realized significant savings. They had been spending a little less than $800 a month but had cut it back to $450 by this time.

There was no stopping us now!

This success motivated us to look at other parts of our budget. We began to find ways to save on everything we needed to buy—a gallon of paint, a new pair of shoes, air filters, pet medications, birthday gifts, movies, even utilities.

We're going to share what we've learned—what we feel everyone should know. Best of all, you get the comprehensive version we were desperately seeking, not the piecemeal version we waded through for our first six months. You won't have to try to figure out what's correct, what's miscommunicated, and what just plain doesn't make a difference.

This book covers four basic areas where we can save more in our daily lives. While illustrating the main methods we use, the first several chapters focus on groceries and personal care products. We spend more time on this topic because for the typical family, this is the biggest chunk of the budget. The next couple of chapters will teach you how to save money around the house on cleaning products and utilities. After that, we'll share tips for saving on all the "other stuff" we have to buy for our families or to maintain our homes: clothing, shoes, gifts, appliances, even vet bills. And in the last two chapters we can start having fun; this is where we'll talk about how to be centsable while you are enjoying entertainment and travel.

At the end of every chapter you will find an action plan. The action plan will help you get started implementing the tips we've outlined. Follow these simple steps to get you going in the right direction. We also suggest that you visit BeCentsable.net for up-to-date links and information. Although some resources are listed in the upcoming chapters, many more are listed on our website so we can be sure they stay current and valuable to you.

We also want to encourage you to take baby steps. We will give you a ton of information in this book, but remember we didn't do everything overnight. We did one thing at a time over the course of a year and a half. And we're still learning, implementing, and refining our skills. We hope that you will use this book as a reference guide. You might want to read the whole book first and then pick the areas you want to start with. Or pick one area to focus on and try out the action plans at the end of that chapter before moving on. However you approach this project it should be a fun challenge. Remember, don't compare yourself to us, your friends, or any other shopper! Do the best you can with what you have. Laugh and learn at the bumps in the road—we hit many along the way—and always, always celebrate your victories!

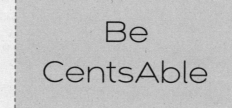

Be
CentsAble

1

Everything You Didn't Know About Coupons

In the Beginning

Before we started on our budget-cutting journey, we rarely used coupons. On the rare occasion we did try to use coupons, we didn't see significant savings. Typically, we'd clip our coupons and throw them in our purse to use later at the store.

Now, everybody knows a purse can be like the Bermuda Triangle; the coupons we threw haphazardly in our bags would never be seen again. Chrissy discovered this the hard way. During one shopping trip, she got up to the register and was ready to pay when she remembered she had brought along some carefully chosen coupons. The cashier and other shoppers stood watching while she frantically dug through her purse to find her coupons. Cell phone, Band-Aids, diaper cream, pacifiers, and pens . . . no coupons. Just then she noticed her one-year-old leaning over the cart, pulling magazines off the rack and trying to tear open the candy. She halted her search and began picking up magazines. She wouldn't be saving any money on this trip!

Our image of the typical coupon user was probably similar to yours: someone ultraorganized, with time to spare, who spent hours on Sunday afternoons cutting and organizing her coupons and knew exactly what was in her file box at any given moment. We suspected coupons would not work for us for many different reasons. At the time, we were both busy moms with two children under the age of two and husbands who worked long hours. We were lucky to find the time to take a shower, let alone find the time to sit down to clip and organize a big stack of coupons. When we did make an honest effort to use coupons we often found store-brand (private-label) products were less expensive than the brand-name products, even with a coupon. In most cases we didn't mind using generic products so we were left thinking coupons would only benefit us on items to which our families were brand loyal. It seemed like the majority of the coupons we came across were for processed foods and other products we did not use. Kristin's son is on a gluten-free diet and Chrissy is a health nut known for bringing low-fat, whole-grain snacks to Super Bowl parties. We both also enjoy cooking from scratch so we incorrectly assumed we would only benefit from coupons on items like household cleaning, toiletries, and personal care products.

As an added nuisance, we sometimes had trouble figuring out which product a given coupon was valid for. We often found ourselves attempting to match up the picture on the coupon with the correct item on the store shelves. As you can imagine, our children sat calmly in the cart while we scrutinized products and coupons! And after all of this hard work, we discovered the average coupon we brought to the store was only worth about 25¢. How could we make a significant budget cut with 25¢ coupons? Was all this hassle and embarrassment, holding up the line and irritating the people behind us, worth saving a few dollars?

The first time Chrissy really tried to use her coupons diligently things did not go well. She got her paper on Sunday morning and spent thirty minutes looking through and cutting out all the coupons her family would use. Once at the store, she put her one-year-old in the cart and slipped her baby in the sling and was off, giddy with the anticipation of saving a load of money. While her one-year-old was trying to "help Mommy" by ripping up all the coupons and the baby was crying for a snack, she tried to compare prices and match up coupons. After spending a *very* long time in the store she found that the store-brand products were less expensive, even with her coupons. When she finally checked out she ended up using only one of the many coupons and saved a whopping 50¢! Had she really wasted thirty minutes cutting out coupons to save 50¢? For a new mom getting only three hours of sleep a night, thirty minutes is extremely valuable. She went home wondering why people waste their time.

We Changed Our Thinking

When we decided to get serious about cutting our budgets we began by asking the experts . . . other parents, our friends, and strangers on the Web! We checked out library books; read forums, websites, and blogs; and flipped through magazines. We read in disbelief about people going to the store and spending only $30 for a cart full of groceries. We started reading about "coupon strategies" people were using as if we were reading a foreign language. We wondered, what is "coupon strategy"? Don't you just cut your coupon out and hand it to the cashier? What could we do differently? Hand the coupon to the cashier with the left hand instead of the right? After several weeks of reading, we realized we had been so wrong! Education is the key. Once we learned how to properly use our coupons those pieces of paper became very valuable to us.

I have to admit that I used to laugh at people who spent so much time using coupons. Why would I spend hours every month cutting and filing coupons to save a few bucks? I felt my time was worth more than the savings I would get. I was surprised to discover I was wrong! Once you learn a few coupon strategies you can save a ton of money. I am so glad I was wrong. Coupons have helped my family cut our budget dramatically.

—Sara

After a lot of reading and research and experimenting, we discovered all our ideas about and experiences with coupons were wrong. We quickly changed our minds about this whole coupon thing. Yes, we admit that we were wrong! Please don't tell our husbands!

> *Myth*
>
> Store-brand products are less expensive than the brand-name varieties even if you use a coupon.

We were ecstatic to discover that we could get brand-name products much cheaper than store-brand varieties, sometimes even for free. Yes, *free*! "Not possible," you say. Well, sit back and keep reading.

We first read about the possibility of free products on a website dedicated to deal seeking. It was one of those "too good to be true" things that we sort of dismissed. But when we read more we continued to see the matter-of-fact claim that not only was it possible, people were actually doing it. Children's Tylenol was the first product we got for free. With the help of our deal-seeking resources online and a strategic combination of store sales, store and manufacturer coupons, and store incentives, we were able to leave the store with over $40 in Children's Tylenol for free, legally (although it didn't feel that way)! As we were heading to our cars that evening, we joked that we better hurry up and get out of the store before someone stopped us.

Once we figured out where to look we found there were coupons available for items our families actually used. There were even coupons for produce, meat, dairy, organics, and all-natural products. We could save money and feed our families healthy (sometimes, even fully organic) meals.

In addition to the inserts in our local Sunday newspapers, we found new sources offering higher value coupons than ones that were in the inserts. Once we knew where to look, it was not uncommon for us to find coupons for $2 or even $3 off a single product. We also learned how to double or even triple the value of our 25¢ coupons that we once thought were a waste of time.

After some practice we found that holding up the grocery store line for two minutes wasn't such a big deal. People behind us in line would even ask us how much we had spent or how we did it. Although we have encountered very few problems when using coupons, there are times when a coupon does not scan or a price does not ring up correctly. One day Chrissy had problems when one of her coupons would not scan and the cashier had to type in the numbers by hand, adding a few seconds to the process. A lady behind her was in a big hurry and was muttering under her breath about the extra time she was taking. This is something that would normally bother Chrissy, but just the day before, she had paid off an extra $250 on her mortgage because of all the money she had saved that month on her groceries. Chrissy walked away with a smile on her face, knowing that one day her house would be paid off early because of coupons!

It is easy to see how the time spent planning and using coupons translated into *meaningful* savings for Chrissy's family. Chrissy would have had to work about thirty-five hours a month (or about nine hours a week) at a part-time job to earn that much "extra money" after taxes. That doesn't account for gas to get to the job or the immeasurable value of her time away from her children and husband. She achieved these savings in much less than half that time and was able to do it while her children were playing or napping.

Once we experienced the power of coupons and how much we could save, we decided coupons were pretty cool; we were no longer skeptical of the savings or embarrassed to use our coupons. We had finally gained control over this part of our budget and realized that smart consumers used coupons.

Coupons 101

Welcome to Coupons 101! Before you can start saving tons of money you first need to learn a few things about using coupons to your advantage. We realize this may seem like high school all over again, but, unlike calculus, you can use this information in real life. Sit back and relax; the bell will ring soon.

Types of Coupons

First things first, you need to know about the different types of coupons. A coupon will clearly state what type it is, typically across the top. If the coupon says the word *manufacturer* on it this means the coupon was created by the manufacturer of the product. You can use a manufacturer's coupon at any store that accepts coupons. A *store* coupon does not have the word "manufacturer" on it but rather it has the name of a specific store on it. Store coupons can only be redeemed at the store that issued the coupon. A Ragú coupon that has "Target" printed at the top can only be redeemed at Target, but a Ragú coupon that has "manufacturer" at the top can be redeemed at any retailer that accepts coupons.

Where to Find Coupons

Next, you need to know where to find coupons. The number one place to find coupons is in the Sunday (or weekend) newspaper. Coupon inserts are distributed by several different companies; the most common are SmartSource, RedPlum, General Mills, Kellogg's, and Procter & Gamble. Some weeks there may only be one insert in your paper while other weeks you may find six different inserts. During the national holiday weekends it is likely that there won't be any coupon inserts in your Sunday paper. It is important to understand the coupon insert schedule so you know when to buy your papers and how many to buy. We recommend that you view a coupon insert schedule (BeCentsable.net posts one) before you buy your Sunday paper.

> $ **Centsable Tip** $
>
> Most local newspapers also include coupon inserts each weekend; subscriptions to these papers can be as much 50% less than the cost of your larger city newspapers.

Printing coupons online is also becoming very popular. Many brand manufacturers are taking advantage of technology to get coupons into consumers' hands at the lowest cost. Some companies will ask you to register with their site to print out coupons. If you choose to do this we suggest you first create a "junk mail" e-mail address with an e-mail service provider, meaning an address that you use only for this purpose. These companies will send you great offers and interesting information but if you don't want your personal or business e-mail address to be overloaded with promotional e-mails, this preemptive step will save your sanity as well as your pocketbook.

We have found that valuable, high-dollar coupons are offered in printable format online more often than they are distributed in newspaper inserts. Manufacturers offer higher value coupons online because they can control the number of times a given person can print the same coupons, they save money on distribution, and the coupons reach their target audience more reliably, so they are more likely to be redeemed.

Printable coupons can be found online at manufacturers' websites and at coupon-aggregating websites run by companies like Coupons, Inc., and RedPlum. We have been very successful finding coupons on manufacturers' websites. We advise everyone to visit their favorite manufacturer's website to see if it offers printable coupons. Go ahead, sign up for its newsletter or register on the site. You may be surprised at what you find in your in-box!

Both of our families love Smart Balance products, so we visited the company's website recently and found $3 worth of printable coupons. Aggregating sites distribute printable coupons for many different brands of products; the manufacturers pay these sites a fee to distribute their coupons in a secure environment. Check these sites often because they typically update their coupon offers every week or so.

Most retail stores will accept online coupons as long as they have the bar code and expiration date printed on them. It is important to use these coupons properly! These coupons may not be photocopied or they will be considered fraudulent. Widespread use of fraudulent coupons can trigger the manufacturer to pull them off the market. When this happens even consumers with legitimate coupons are not able to redeem them. Please be a responsible consumer, and teach others to be as well!

To print online coupons, all you need is a computer and printer. This is simple, free, and fast. The first time you print a coupon from a given website you may be prompted to download a "coupon printer." This is simply a small program that tells your computer how to print the bar code properly so it can be scanned at the store. Your computer will alert you to the request and guide you through the process. The programs installed by the sites we mention in this book or link to from our website are widely used and regarded as safe. However, any time you download files from the Internet, you should have up-to-date virus protection installed and active on your computer. Most sites will allow you to print two copies of the same coupon.

> **$ Centsable Tip $**
>
> When printing coupons online be sure to set your printer to print in black and white to save money.

After you print the first coupon, you can simply hit the BACK button a couple of times until the coupon is resent to your printer. If a notice that your print limit has been reached appears for a coupon you have not printed, you can assume that means the coupon is not available in your region any longer. To print additional copies of a specific coupon after the print limit has been reached, check back at a later date. Often after a couple of weeks, the coupon limits are reset by the manufacturer and you can print the coupon again. Recently we experienced this with coupons for Honey Bunches of Oats cereal. We were able to go to Post's website and print out two

$2 off coupons. A few weeks later the company reset the print limits and we printed two more. Over a six-month period we were able to print these coupons four different times; that's eight coupons!

The majority of the coupons we use are from newspapers or online, but there are many other valuable sources. For example, community fund-raising coupon books are a great find. Many local grocery stores offer these coupon books to nonprofit community and school groups to sell. This is a great way to support your community because the profit goes directly to the organization selling the books. Most of the time, a single coupon in these books covers the cost of the entire book ($5 or $10 off your grocery purchase). It is important to check to see if these coupons are store coupons or manufacturer coupons. Remember, if they specify "manufacturer" coupon on them you can redeem them at any retailer that accepts coupons.

Another great place to look for coupons is on the product itself. These coupons are called "peelies" because you can peel them off and redeem them the same day. These coupons are only meant to be removed at the time you are buying the product. Please do not turn into the crazy person at the store peeling off all the coupons on the Huggies diapers. We don't want to be talking about you when we can't find a package with a coupon intact!

Another often overlooked resource is direct home mailers. These are product information pamphlets that often include coupons. They come by postal mail and can be an easy way to collect coupons for product brands your family uses. We suggest contacting any manufacturer whose products you use on a regular basis or want to try. When we both had two little ones in diapers we contacted Huggies, Pampers, and Luvs to get on their mailing lists. In many cases, once you get on their mailing list the coupons keep coming. Last but not least, magazines like *All You* are offering an increasing number of coupons to their readers. *All You* magazine is one we recommend and use often. Each issue usually offers over $50 worth of coupons!

Organizing Our Coupons

Now that you know the different types of coupons and where to find them you need to learn how to organize your coupons. Organization is a key part of cutting our budget. We have to admit that we are both organizing junkies at heart but have little time to follow through. That's why we love our coupon filing method: little time, big results!

Don't Repeat Our Mistake

Remember that golden rule of organizing, "Touch it once," meaning you put things where they belong as soon as they come into the house? Well, for a while our practice when it came to filing coupons was more like "Touch it as many times as possible before you actually use it." What a waste of time!

Before we found the key to our coupon filing sanity, our coupon filing "systems" could go on a list of what not to do. Kristin used to "organize" her coupons by clipping them and systematically arranging them into neat little piles all around her kitchen. First she would take the inserts out of the Sunday paper and place them on the microwave. A few days later she would clip the coupons out. Several days later she would finally get around to sorting them into several piles. This system worked great until she forgot where she was in the process of sorting and filing and how her piles were organized. Was it by food type or by brand? She would be all ready to go to the store and could not find the coupon she was looking for. She had a coupon for coffee in one of her piles, but which one? After thirty minutes of looking through all the piles a second (or even third) time she realized that it was not worth the dollar she was trying to save. Of course she would find the coupon the next day under her coffee cup.

Chrissy, on the other hand, carefully clipped her coupons and filed them in a small file box (at least one time, anyway). The only opportunity she had to organize her coupons was on Sunday nights with her one-year-old daughter at her side helping her. More than once, she found the baby was eating coupons or snagging the file box and dumping the whole thing on the floor. By the time Chrissy got around to refiling her coupons, most of them had expired.

> ### *Myth*
> Clipping, sorting, and filing coupons takes too much time.

If you can't find your coupons or it takes forever to file them, you are wasting your time. You will be frustrated, unmotivated, and unlikely to use those valuable pieces of paper. At the beginning of our journey we were learning how valuable coupons were but lacked an organization system that worked for us. For most consumers, the biggest hurdle to using coupons is the time it takes to find them. No doubt there are numerous ways to organize and file coupons. We will outline below the method we love for its simplicity and speed and mention a few other options later in this section.

Lucky for us, early on in our journey we read about a coupon filing method, or system, created by Stephanie Nelson, which eliminates all that time spent clipping, sorting, and filing. We've used it and loved it since day one! We're going to share it with you and walk through the process. It keeps us organized so we can take full advantage of all of the great deals without tearing our hair out.

As we promised in the beginning, this will save valuable time, time you can use planning your shopping trip, creating menus, and counting up all the money you are saving. We call this a "virtual" filing system because all of the sorting and filing is done on the Internet. The coupons are sorted, filed, and cross-referenced by whatever criteria you choose with a simple click of the mouse. All that's left for you to do is clip the coupon when you are ready to go to the store.

At first, we were hesitant to try this system because we thought nothing could be so easy. However, once we tried it we were believers! It gave us the organization we craved without the time commitment. No more clipping, sorting, filing, resorting (oops, that one is expired), sorting some more. Now when we plan our trips we make a list of all the coupons we need and clip only the coupons we will use on shopping day. This takes us only about five minutes. Now Kristin has time to sit down and have a cup of coffee without finding any coupons sticking to her coffee cup.

I would like to thank you for showing me the light at the end of the couponing tunnel. I am so glad that you have taught me the virtual filing system. This has allowed me to use and organize my coupons more than I thought I ever could. As for looking up the coupons it could not be easier. When I have my grocery list ready, all I do is type in the product name and there is my coupon. It's so simple, no searching or thumbing through stacks of coupons anymore. I can't bear to see anyone keep their coupons any other way. Thanks for saving me time and making my life easier.

—Tayler

How to Set Up a Virtual Filing System

MATERIALS NEEDED:

- Expanding box file or large three-ring binder
- Page protectors
- Permanent marker or small labels
- Divider tabs (optional)

1. Remove the inserts from the newspaper. It may be helpful to glance through the coupons each week but you *do not* need to clip them.
2. Label the front of the insert (or use the address labels) with the date shown on the spine of the inserts (this will correspond to the date of the newspaper the inserts were distributed with).
3. Last, slip them in a page protector to keep them together and file them in date order. Place them in the binder or the expanding file. You may wish to use divider tabs to separate the inserts by month.

Now that the inserts are filed away you need to know how to find the coupons when you need them. To do this we use publicly available coupon databases on the Internet. They are free and comprehensive. To look up your coupons in the virtual database on the Web we recommend accessing a widely used database like www. hotcouponworld.com (view a list of all the databases available at BeCentsable.net). These sites require you to register to access the listings, but this is free and we don't see other communications from them. Once registered, log in and click the "Coupon Database" button. Enter the item you are looking for, either by product name, category, or brand, to see if there are any coupons available and from which insert.

If we were looking for Dannon yogurt we would first enter "Dannon"; if there were no results we would try "yogurt." The results will indicate the coupon type (store or manufacturer); product details (e.g., Dannon Activia); and where the coupon can be found, such as in a Sunday newspaper insert (6/21 SS), or online on the company's website.

Our site, BeCentsable.net, like other money-saving resource sites, not only shares what the deals are that week but where to find the coupons. For example, our site may show that Target is having a deal on Kellogg's cereal for $1.58 a box and there is a coupon for $1.50 off in the 3/16 SS. To find this coupon we would go to our coupon file and pull out the March 16 SmartSource insert (or inserts), flip through a few pages, and clip the coupon.

The really great thing about this method of filing and notating coupons is that it's universal; nearly everyone will be using the same system so you can search around the Web and not feel like you need to learn a foreign language to do it!

COUPON INSERT ABBREVIATIONS

GM: General Mills
KG: Kellogg's
PG: Procter & Gamble
RP: RedPlum
SS: SmartSource

After we've gone over this section with our workshop attendees we often get this question: "Why would I want to save *all* the coupons and what should I do with the ones I will not use?"

Glad you asked! First, being a smart consumer is sometimes about being flexible as well. There are some things we would not normally buy but are willing to substitute when the price is right. Having the stash of miscellaneous coupons helps us get the most for our money.

Second, but very close to our hearts, we can help people in our community who need it.

We can help military families stationed overseas by sending our unused or expired coupons to the base commissaries for distribution. We can help them *and thank them* by offering this small substitution for the great deals they could get here in the States. Families stationed at bases outside the United States can use expired coupons in the commissary for up to six months past their expiration date. It requires considerable resources to move your family to another country and, as we can only imagine, there is a limit to the things that can be shipped.

> $ **Centsable Tip** $
>
> Visit the Overseas Coupon Project (a nonprofit orga-
> nization) at www.ocpnet.org to find out how to send
> your unused or expired coupons to military families
> stationed overseas.

We also save all our coupons in case there is a great deal on an item that our family will not use. So why would we get an item that our family will not use? Simply because it is on sale? No! We can give it to charity and help out other families! Imagine if you could take $5 and turn it into $15. We often go the store and use coupons to purchase items at rock-bottom prices, then we give them to charity. Charities run on very limited budgets and doing this small service helps them stretch their funds further. Kristin was able to donate over $160 worth of brand-name groceries, toiletries, and personal care products to one of her local food pantries last Christmas for only $26! This is a great way to give back to your community even if you are on a tight budget.

How to File Your Loose Coupons

Despite our best efforts, and using a virtual coupon filing system, we always have some loose coupons floating around. Many of them come to us as direct-mail pieces, from companies we registered with or requested coupons from; some are a result of last-minute substitutions or changes in the midst of shopping or were unused because the store was out of stock on the item. We use a small portable organizer to file these coupons. Since the majority of our coupons are from the Sunday paper and we file them virtually, we only have a small number of loose coupons to organize. When selecting a loose coupon organizer, we suggest that you look for one that has a place for a shopping list, credit cards, and store loyalty cards and maybe even a pen and calculator.

If you prefer to clip, sort, and file all of your coupons from the Sunday inserts, there are several options available to you for filing them and keeping them organized. We have come across a myriad of methods, from shoe boxes with envelopes and index card dividers to binders with baseball card holders, and everything in between. What matters is that the system works for you. It has to be something that is manageable within your family's lifestyle.

Whatever method you choose, we suggest you have a sturdy, sizable organizer and set time aside every week to clip, sort, and file. Some shoppers prefer the opportunity to see all of the coupons they have in their file and have a good memory when it comes time to make a list. We do not have good memories (let's just call it "mommy brain"). The virtual databases will still be a valuable resource when you are looking for and planning your shopping. You will be able to look up items and see if there is a valid coupon in your area. This may help you save some time flipping through your coupons for each and every item.

Stacking Your Savings

All our coupons are organized, and now we need to know how to use them. There is so much more to using a coupon than just presenting it at the checkout. As we mentioned before, there are actually coupon strategies that will help you use your coupons to their fullest potential. The most important strategy to understand is *timing*. The key to this process is *when* to redeem your coupons. Timing is essential to fully maximizing your savings. The manufacturers' strategy is to create brand loyalty by enticing you to purchase its product. The manufacturers want consumers to redeem coupons right away. They want us to go to the store and buy their brand simply because we have a coupon. And the following week, when we are at the store again, the manufacturers are betting that we will pick up their product again because we loved it.

A centsable shopper waits to "stack" her savings by using her coupons when the sale prices are in effect. "Stacking" refers to using more than one coupon or strategy to get a single product at a rock-bottom price. One of the first products we bought this way was ricotta cheese. Chrissy had several ricotta cheese coupons for $1.00 off. Ricotta cheese is typically $3.79 at her local grocery store. She waited six weeks to use the coupon, when the cheese was on sale for $2.00 each. With her $1.00 off coupon, she paid just

$1.00 for this product. This is a savings of 74%. Since she had six coupons, she bought six and froze five of them to use later. If she hadn't waited for the sale, she would have paid $2.79 for the ricotta cheese, only 26% off.

Once we learned how to time our coupons the savings really started to add up. Remember the $2 off Honey Bunches of Oats coupons we mentioned earlier? Every time we printed those coupons we waited for a sale, and every time, several weeks after we printed our coupons, we would catch this cereal on sale for $2. With our coupon and the sale, we were getting the cereal for *free*! See how powerful timing can be?

Since starting to shop the BeCentsable way in November of 2008, I have saved hundreds of dollars and have a lot of success stories to tell. My favorite, however, is when Hen House was having a sale on Quaker Instant Oatmeal (my kids' favorite) and Purex laundry soap (doing laundry for 7 means I use a lot of this stuff). As the cashier totaled my purchase I noted the amount before my coupons—$56.72. Then came the time for redemption—of my coupons, that is! My loyalty shopper card applied the sale price to the items, which I timed with the coupons I printed from the Internet. By using these combined methods my total price came down to $4.53. The cashier (who I might mention was in training) was speechless—he looked at the total again and then said, "I need to call the manager. I have done something really wrong!" I laughed and said, "No, no, you didn't do anything wrong—I did something totally right!" I was so excited as I left the store that I could have done cartwheels through the parking lot!

—*Beth*

In order to achieve Beth's savings, we need to know when the item we are buying is at the store's lowest sale price, or "rock-bottom price," and if we have coupons to match. To determine if the item is at its rock bottom, we need to keep a price book and log the prices of that item for about six months. Once we see the product is at a good price we need to check for matching coupons. This process would take a lot of time and effort, especially for someone just getting started, but there is an easier way! There are money-saving websites and blogs where the work is done for you. On our site, www.becentsable.net, we maintain a listing of these resources you can refer to any time you are planning a weekly shopping trip. We will go over how this saves time in chapter 4, on planning.

> When I went to my BeCentsable workshop, I thought I was pretty knowledgeable about coupons and savings. Boy, I had no idea how wrong I was. I learned from the workshop many strategies but the one that was so meaningful was coupon timing. I learned that I could save so much more money by just waiting for the items I use to go on sale and then using my coupon. I practice coupon timing every week now and save hundreds of dollars for our household budget. An example I recently used was brand-name spaghetti sauce that regularly cost $2.50. The sauce was on sale for 99¢ and I had two coupons for 30¢ off each, so my final cost was 69¢ per jar. That was a savings of $1.81 per jar. I am so thankful for learning how to help my family save money!
>
> —*Emma*

Another way to stack your savings is to *use more than one coupon* on one item. Earlier in the chapter we discussed how there are manufacturer and store coupons. These coupons come from two different sources so they can be combined to buy one product. It is important to know that you can only use a store coupon and a manufacturer coupon together, and not two store coupons or two manufacturer coupons. For example, Kristin found a store coupon from Walgreens for 50¢ off Kleenex tissues and she also had a manufacturer coupon for 50¢ off. Walgreens had a box of Kleenex tissues on sale for $1 and since she had two 50¢ off coupons she got the item for free.

Many stores also offer coupons that say when you buy a specified dollar amount, you get a specified dollar amount back. These are called "X off of X" coupons, and they are powerful because we can stack them with other store or manufacturer coupons to save even more money. For example, Chrissy recently had a coupon for $5 off of a $20 purchase at her local grocery store. She knew that a box of Pampers diapers was $20 and she had a $5 off coupon for a box of Pampers. She was able to stack both coupons together to get her box of diapers for only $10.

$ **Centsable Tip** $

Remember that order matters! You must give the cashier the "X off of X" coupon first. If you gave him the manufacturer coupon first, your total might fall below the purchase amount specified by the "X off of X" coupon.

The Power of Stacking

Stacking can help you get unbelievable deals and all it takes is a little creativity. Once you have mastered the art of timing your coupons with sales and understand how to use more than one coupon on an item then you are ready to move on to more complicated stacking strategies. After a few months of stacking sales and coupons, we decided to take our stacking strategies to the next level. We found PetSmart had store coupons for $10 off a $30 purchase. Since this was a blanket coupon for a purchase of virtually anything in the store, it became an additional stacking option separate from any sales or store coupons on specific items. We used this strategy when PetSmart had many Iams products on sale for $30, plus it was offering a store coupon for Iams products, and we had Iams manufacturer coupons. We got a forty-eight-pound bag of dog food for only $7. Here is what the deal looked like:

1 bag (48 lbs.) Iams dog food ($30)
Total before coupons = $30
– $10 off $30 purchase (PetSmart store coupon)
– $8 off (Iams manufacturer coupon)
– $5 off (Iams PetSmart coupon)
Final price = $7 + tax

> **$ Centsable Tip $**
>
> Don't try to stack more than two strategies or coupons until you have practiced some basic coupon strategies first.

Just when you think it can't get any better, it does! Coupons can also be stacked with store incentives like price matching, store credit, and rebates. We will cover store incentives in the next chapter.

Action Plan

As you have read in this chapter, coupons can be valuable and do not have to take a ton of time. We encourage you to keep an open you mind as change your way of thinking about coupons and saving money. Let coupons give your budget that kick it needs.

1. Choose a filing system. Will you use the virtual system, or clip and file all of your paper coupons?
   a. For virtual systems you need:
      i. File box or three-ring binder.
      ii. An organizer that you take to the store that will hold the coupons you plan to use on that shopping trip, plus any loose coupons (printables, and those from magazines, mailers, etc.) you have lying around.
   b. If you are planning to clip, sort, and file your coupons, you will need:
      i. An organizer that you use to file all your coupons and a small one that you can take to the store.
2. Get a Sunday paper and start your coupon file.
3. Go online and print off a few coupons to practice. Go to BeCentsable.net for a list of websites.
4. Check out BeCentsable.net for:
   a. Coupon insert schedules.
   b. Lists of virtual coupon databases.

2

Store Types, Store Incentive Programs, and How to Use Both Effectively

Finding great deals doesn't mean you have to rely on manufacturers to distribute coupons. Sometimes it simply means knowing where and how to shop. Just as manufacturers offer coupons and rebates to encourage consumers to buy their products, stores also offer coupons, sales, specials, and other incentives to consumers to spend money with them. Every store we visit can be placed in one of three basic categories. These categories will tell you a lot about what to expect from the weekly sales ads and how or even if you should shop at a particular store.

In this chapter we will explain each store type, talk about the different incentives each one offers to their customers, and explain how to make the most of them. We'll also debunk a few myths and hopefully encourage you to try out some stores you were avoiding.

Everyday Low Price Stores

The biggest selection of goods can be found at stores in the category we like to call *everyday low*. These stores have buying power and it shows! They offer a wide array of goods from groceries and personal care to clothing, electronics, and furniture. They are able to keep prices low because these chains negotiate the best deals with manufacturers by buying in very large quantities.

Stores in this category do not offer regular weekly sales specials. Everyday low price stores are more likely to have a few items on clearance each week when the store needs to make room for new products or upcoming seasonal inventory. Consumers purchasing goods at stores in this category are taking advantage of a built-in incentive: economies of scale. These stores use their low prices to attract an enormous customer base, which they use as a negotiating tool to continue buying and selling at the lowest prices.

Myth

There are no extra savings to be found at an everyday low price store; their prices are already the lowest around.

In order to maintain the low-price distinction and customer loyalty, these stores sometimes offer a *price match guarantee* to their shoppers. Price matching is an additional incentive program customers can take advantage of to save money. The retailer offers this because it knows it can achieve a higher return by offering savings to a few satisfied customers than it can by selling fewer products at higher prices. Shoppers can usually price-match any of their local stores, even discount grocers, within a specified radius of each store location (this varies with the size of the city and concentration of stores in the area). This incentive is *easy to use* and you don't even need to go to the customer service counter!

Don't Repeat Our Mistake

Don't be afraid to take advantage of price match-ing and other special store incentives because you think people will be annoyed with you. We cringe at the number of years we avoided price matching at our local store because we didn't want to inconve-nience anyone.

The first time Chrissy price-matched she was very nervous it would be a huge ordeal. She had visions of the manager coming over to the register and taking her to a back room. The manager would shine a light in her face and ask, "So you think you can get this cheaper someplace else?" She was pleasantly surprised when all she had to do was tell the cashier that she had an item to price-match. The cashier just smiled and said, "Okay, what's the price?" It only took about thirty seconds. Chrissy couldn't believe how easy it was and was excited to try it again.

Below are some price-matching tips to keep in mind. These apply to most everyday low stores with a price-matching program.

1. Remember to bring the competitor's sales flyer. Some of the everyday low chains keep current store ads in a central loca-tion at the registers. You won't be asked to show proof very often but in the event you are, it will be easier if you have the competitor's ad with you.

2. Items you wish to price-match must be the exact item in the competitor's ad (size, variety or flavor, and quantity).

3. You can only price-match items advertised with a specific

dollar amount. Most stores will not allow you to match percentage-off sales or "buy one, get one" offers.

4. Remember to go through a regular checkout (no self-checking when you want to price-match).

5. Keep items you plan to price-match separate when you check out (either at the beginning or the end of your transaction). This just helps you and the cashier keep things more organized.

We recently price-matched a six-pack of yogurt, typically $2.89, that was on sale at a local grocery store for $1.50. Price matching is our favorite strategy when we are in a hurry and have little time. It allows us to take advantage of deals from multiple stores in only one stop. With a little bit of planning a centsable shopper can save time and money at everyday low price stores (we'll go over planning tips and tricks later in the book).

Kristin was able to save more than half of her grocery bill using a simple price-matching program available at her local store. The week before Thanksgiving she purchased everything she needed for a holiday dinner for her family and a few friends, as well as some extras for the week after so they wouldn't have to go out shopping again, and she only had to visit one store to take advantage of all the great deals. With just $10 in coupons she saved over $100 by taking advantage of price matching.

> $ **Centsable Tip** $
>
> Don't forget that you can use coupons when you price-match to save even more money!

One drawback to an everyday low store is the size, variety, and selection of certain products. Because these stores are looking to pay, and offer, the lowest possible price on a product, they often have unique sizes and varieties. The selection may be limited to the most popular variety of a certain product, or the product you want could be packaged with a promotional item (like a free sample of lotion when you purchase a bottle of sunscreen) or be sold only in larger volume containers. This can make using coupons and price matching a little more difficult and, at times, result in lost savings or force consumers to purchase substitute products that we wouldn't typically choose to buy.

Another potential drawback is the fact that everyday low price stores have an array of consumer goods that rivals any other store type. It's easy to wander the store (assuming you do not have your screaming toddler with you) to see if there is anything else you might need and end up wasting away your savings with impulse purchases. While we cannot control your impulse purchases we do have a few shopping tips we'll go over later in chapter 5.

High/Low Stores

The next category is the most prevalent and can also be the most difficult for shopping and saving money despite the fact that nearly every consumer frequents one of these stores on a weekly basis. The *high/low* category includes almost every grocery store and drugstore and they all follow the same basic incentive pattern. High/low stores tend to have higher regular prices than everyday low price stores on most items but offer shoppers deep discounts on a few selected items each week, called "loss leaders." As the name might suggest, the store is taking a loss on a handful of items to get shoppers in the door. Most consumers will do all of their shopping at one store each week, so once they are in the door, they take advantage of the loss leader that got them there and pay the regular, slightly higher prices on the rest of the products they need for the week. You will find the loss leaders from store to store are basically the same but beyond that there is a wide range of prices.

Myth

You will find the lowest prices on groceries at a grocery store. It's their specialty!

A definite benefit to shopping these stores is they have a wide selection within their specialty (for example, groceries, health and natural foods, drugs and personal care, and pet care) and frequently offer in-store specials or unadvertised sales as a simple incentive to shoppers.

High/low grocery stores are becoming more competitive with one another and with the everyday low price stores. As a result, they are developing some very valuable incentive programs to earn customer loyalty. The incentives range from the basic (using your loyalty card to get advertised savings and coupons) to the more complex (buy two pounds of chicken and get $5 off your next shopping trip), attracting both the random customer as well as the returning customer.

$ **Centsable Tip** $

At grocery stores, store credit offers usually come in the form of catalinas, named for the company that developed the software to print and distribute them. Catalinas are coupons that you can use on your next visit. These coupons are printed at the register at the end of your transaction.

A great incentive more and more stores are offering is *double coupon* days or even double coupons every day! Coupon doubling is almost exclusively offered by grocery stores. "Double coupons" simply refers to the practice of doubling the value of a single coupon when it is redeemed at the register. If you have a coupon for 50¢ off, it would automatically double at the register to $1 off. Remember, you can stack your double coupons with sale prices! A good example of how we use coupon doubling to cut our grocery expenses is a recent purchase of Smart Balance products that we made. Our local grocery store was offering the entire line of Smart Balance products on sale for $1.75 each. We had accumulated several 50¢ off coupons that we could stack with the sale price. Since all the products were on sale for $1.75 and our 50¢ off coupons would be doubled (for a total of $1.00 off per product) we paid just 75¢ for each one. Since Smart Balance products are typically upwards of $3.00 (and sometimes more), we stocked up!

It is important to note that stores offering this incentive will usually place restrictions and limits on the coupon value and quantity. It's important to ask about double-coupon policies at your store so you can make the most of the opportunity.

Don't Repeat Our Mistake

Don't get stuck in a rut going to the same store every week because you think the prices are pretty much the same everywhere. Even after several months of shopping "centsably," we discovered a store in the town next to ours that doubled coupons every day! It was the only one in our area that did this. We just hadn't ventured outside our comfort zone. It does matter which store you go to, and prices vary wildly from store to store in the high/low category.

What if we told you that you could get $100 worth of items for $10 or you could get free toothpaste, razors, makeup, and deodorant? Well, you can! We haven't paid for shampoo, conditioner, toothpaste, or soap for two years. No, we haven't stop taking showers; we just started shopping at drugstores. High/low drugstores are evolving to attract shoppers from some of the big national chains by offering powerful store incentives.

Their incentive programs are valuable but sometimes complex. The trick here is learning exactly how these programs work and how to make the most of them. Take the time; it can be extremely beneficial to your pocketbook—to the tune of hundreds of dollars' worth of free products each year. When we first learned how to use these drugstore incentives we were so astonished at how much we could save that we would come home and lay out our deals for our husbands to guess how much we spent. We often had $50 worth of items that we paid less than $5 for.

> I would never shop at drugstores because I assumed they were more expensive. Boy, was I ever wrong! Once I learned how to use their store incentive programs I started getting things very cheap and sometimes even free! On my last visit I got $80 worth of items for $10.69!
>
> *—Ruth*

Because these programs are relatively new, stores are still learning and changing the details and policies along the way. Since drugstores are constantly changing their incentive programs we will not teach you what each store's current incentive plan is but we will teach you how to utilize the basic components of these programs. Drugstore incentive programs have three components: store coupons, store credit, and rebates. The complicated part about this is that each store may use the same incentive but with different rules and requirements. For example, two drugstores might issue store credit but both programs are different, so you have to learn how each one works to be able to take full advantage. At both stores you purchase some specific dollar amount or combination of products and at the checkout you will receive your store credit. At one store you may receive your store credit in the form of a store gift card and at another you might receive your store credit in the form of a coupon. The store credit that comes in the form of a gift card never expires and can be used on anything in the store. The store credit that comes in the form of a coupon must be used in two to four weeks and includes restrictions on what you can buy. The coupon usually doesn't allow you to receive cash back, so if you have money left over you lose it, unlike the gift card, where the money remains on the card until it's gone.

Store coupons are a very popular incentive that most drug-stores utilize. The difference here is where to find the store coupons. Some stores will have store coupons in their print ads, while others only make theirs available online or by e-mail. Refer back to chapter 1 for more information on store coupons and how to use them.

Rebate programs are another common store incentive. Rebates can be usually redeemed online or through the mail. You typically pay for an item up front and then submit your rebate to get cash back in the form of a check or store gift card. Once again, it is important to understand how your store's incentive plan works. Some stores make their rebates available for the whole month while other stores may only make them available for a week.

Don't forget to stack! Remember from the last chapter how to stack your coupons together to get rock-bottom prices? Well, you can use coupons with all these store incentives to get products for very little or even free. We recently stacked manufacturer coupons with store credit offers to walk away with $37.41 worth of items for free. Here is what the deal looked like:

2 Excedrin (100 ct.) $6.99 each
6 Speed Stick $1.99 each
1 Eye shadow $5.49
2 Huggies swim diapers $3.00 each
Total = $37.41

COUPONS USED:

$5.00 off $30.00 purchase
2 $3.00 off Excedrin
3 $1.00 off Speed Stick
2 $1.50 off Huggies
Total savings: $17.00
Total out of pocket (store credit): $20.41

$ **Centsable Tip** $

Does this sound too complicated? Don't worry, we have a solution! We are two busy moms who don't have time to sit and analyze sales ads, so we let other people do the work for us. In chapter 4, on planning, we will show you how to find all these great deals without doing any work.

Does this sound too good to be true? We didn't believe it either, until we started doing deals like this every month (sometimes even every week). This is just one of the many, many examples of great drugstore deals you can take advantage of. Be sure to take the time to learn how your local drugstores' incentive plans work!

Wholesale Clubs

"So I pay the store to let me shop there? Ummm, I'm not interested."

Okay, well, yes, you do pay the store, but you pay it to let you *save* there! And you're saving as a centsable shopper now. Nothing to fear, we'll make it worthwhile.

Although the first wholesale club was opened in the United States in the 1950s, wholesale clubs as we know them came into being in the 1980s with the opening of BJ's Wholesale Club. The three chains operating today, BJ's, Sam's Club, and Costco, are growing in popularity.

The concern we hear most often when choosing to become a member of a wholesale club is recouping the annual fees. Annual household membership fees range from $30 to $50 and are a big reason why consumers don't take advantage of the savings available at wholesale clubs.

Toss that excuse out the window! Below we will tell you how to shop at a wholesale club, identify which foods are typically a centsable buy, and demonstrate how you can save four times the cost of that annual membership by purchasing one product!

Myth

Wholesale club memberships aren't worth the annual fee.

Wholesale clubs serve a couple of purposes: manufacturers can sell off overstock product, and small business owners can take advantage of buying in bulk. If you've ever shopped at a wholesale club you know if you see something you really want, you'd better grab it or it will likely be gone next time you're there. This is the case for nearly all textiles, appliances, décor, electronics, and specialty items they carry. The stock is limited and if the price is right, you can bet the product will sell through its stock pretty quickly. This is what brings a lot of traffic through the doors, so wholesale clubs also offer a steady inventory of nondurable goods (food, office supplies, books, movies, etc.) to keep traffic flowing on a regular basis.

A wholesale club is itself an incentive program. Buying power alone can save you 10%–20% on the items you purchase. The average grocery store operates on a 20%–50% markup, averaging around 40%. Wholesale clubs operate at an 8%–15% markup. In addition to low prices, several of the wholesale clubs we've visited offer their members an unrivaled return policy with few restrictions. Kristin and her husband recently returned a broken four-year-old digital camera they'd purchased at Sam's Club, and the store replaced it with a *new* one, for free. They received a full price credit on the broken camera to apply to the purchase of a new one—not a refurbished camera and not one of similar quality, but a brand-new, much better digital camera. In most cases, this policy applies to everything but computers. Add to that the high-quality, low-cost private-label products and the additional monthly or quarterly member coupon savings and you've got a reason to visit a wholesale club.

Recouping Your Membership Fees

First, you only want to buy items at a wholesale club that your family already uses on a regular basis or that can be stored dry or frozen and used over the course of several months. If you go to the wholesale club and purchase a cartful of things you don't typically buy or that may spoil in a couple of weeks, you definitely won't save money!

WHAT SHOULD YOU LOOK FOR AT A WHOLESALE CLUB?
ASK YOURSELF THESE THREE QUESTIONS:

1. Is it something my family uses daily (e.g., milk, cheese, yogurt, bread, toilet paper)?
2. Is it something I can easily store in my home? If not, can I split it with a friend or family member?
3. Is it *really* a good deal?

First, is this something your family uses on a regular basis? If you aren't in desperate need of a tube of toothpaste the day you are at the store, it doesn't make sense to purchase it at a wholesale club. Yes, the tubes are small and storage is not really a concern but you can get toothpaste at amazing discounts at your local drugstores fairly frequently, so purchasing it in bulk at a slightly lower than retail price is not going to help you in the long run. Likewise, when you see a phenomenal deal on something, if your family won't use it up in six months or less, you should think twice about the purchase. Save that space in your pantry for something more valuable or a higher savings item.

The reason for not shopping at wholesale clubs we hear most frequently, after concerns about recouping membership fees, is lack of storage space. We have to be honest, that was one of our primary concerns, too. This is an issue to give some thought to as you are walking through the store; that, and fitting it all in your car!

Don't Repeat Our Mistake

Think, think, think, and plan ahead! Chrissy and I took all four of our children (ages two and under) on a major shopping trip to our favorite wholesale club one morning only to discover we didn't have the manpower or the vehicle space to get what we needed!

We did serve up some entertainment for our fellow shoppers when we tried to maneuver two forty-four-pound bags of dog food into our carts while each carrying an infant in our baby carriers. When we got to our cars, we realized neither of us really had room for all of the stuff we had bought. We spent more time reorganizing the vehicles and splitting food than we did in the store.

It's worth it to discuss going to the wholesale club with your friends and family. Perhaps someone is looking to take advantage of a membership but is assessing these same concerns and would be interested in splitting the membership costs with your family, or maybe they just want to split food occasionally. This arrangement could save everyone involved a lot of money down the road. We used to shop at our wholesale clubs together. We would split packages of food our families would use but did not have room for or would not be able to eat through before it spoiled, especially freezer goods and produce.

Finally, consider whether or not the item you're about to purchase is *really* a good deal. This will take time to learn. As you shop each week, start taking notes on the prices of items you buy most often, picking one or two to focus on each week. When you are at the wholesale club, look at the price and the size of the packages. Wholesale clubs like to break prices down into unit cost for you but sometimes the unit size has nothing to do with how you use the product. Really, who knows how many ounces are in a gallon of milk? You'll need to pay attention to the size of the product you typically buy and compare that to the size of the product you will be buying at the wholesale club. For example, if you normally spend $2.00 on a one-pound loaf of bread at the grocery store and you see you can get two one-and-a-half-pound loaves at the wholesale club for $3.50, you can easily see that this is a bargain. And if you do the math, you confirm it: that's 84¢ less per pound.

$ **Centsable Tip** $

It's an accepted activity with club members to pop into their local store for free lunch or dinner! Wholesale clubs are renowned for their extensive sampling activity and the food is yummy. Enjoy! But keep a strong will. *Do not* pick up the package of food you just sampled! It may be good, but unless it's already on your list, it will eat up your savings every time.

Listed below are broad categories of foods that are typically less expensive (when compared to national chains and your local grocery store) at a wholesale club. Remember, this varies slightly from region to region. Pay attention to prices at the grocery store next time you are there or save a few receipts to compare while you are shopping.

- Dairy
- Grains (but not always cereal)

- Some produce (this category can be difficult because of regional variations in crop seasons)
- Paper products
- Canned meats
- Condiments and spreads (especially honey, peanut butter, maple syrup, jelly)
- Organics in the categories already listed

Okay, here is a quick demonstration of how easy it is to recoup the cost of an annual wholesale club membership.

The average family of four buys three gallons of milk a week. For us it's more like seven or eight gallons a week. With as much milk as our families use we have often thought it would just be cheaper to put a cow in the backyard. Maybe then we could stop mowing the yard, too.

Anyhow, we've found that the average price for a gallon of milk at the grocery or chain store is $2.69. At three gallons a week the average family is spending $420 a year on milk. The average price of a gallon of milk at a wholesale club is $1.49 a gallon (seriously, this is what we are paying for milk), just $232 a year. Quick, get a calculator. . . .

You save 45% on your milk and recoup your $50 membership cost nearly four times over! And that's just one product!

Add to this the amazing, free guarantee and returns policy and we have some very strong incentives to visit the wholesale club.

Regardless of where you shop, it's important to be familiar with the incentives offered by other stores in your area. You can take advantage of the occasional "can't pass it up" deal if you are just slightly familiar with all the store incentives. It also helps to get to know your regional prices on produce, dairy, meats, and grains. These are the items whose prices tend to fluctuate most often due to demand and their shorter shelf life. You will no doubt find great deals on pantry items and frozen foods, but you have to be observant and diligent to ensure you aren't overpaying for fresh foods and perishables.

Incentives That Apply to Every Store

Although this chapter is focused on specific store incentives, there are a few that span across stores, usually because they are offered directly by manufacturers.

Manufacturer Rebates

We mentioned store rebate programs earlier and you will remember those programs are offered and administered exclusively by an individual store. There are also rebates available to anyone shopping at any store during the offer period. These rebates are offered by the manufacturer. Rebates are pretty quick and easy; there are just a few things to know.

1. Be sure to note exactly which product you are required to purchase to earn the rebate.
2. Be sure to read the offer thoroughly before you go shopping. Every rebate offer is different, and if you don't follow the details precisely you will not get that money back.
3. Double-check the offer dates and the submission dates. The offer may be good for six months (meaning you have six months in which to make the purchase) and you may have thirty days beyond that to get your rebate request mailed to the manufacturer or you may only have until the last day of the offer to mail the request.

4. Did we mention you should read the offer thoroughly before going shopping?

We have to admit we don't send in a lot of rebate requests . . . "mommy brain" again! Rebates can be really great when you find one for a product your family will use. For example, when we first began using coupons and researching great deals we came across a rebate offer from a program called the Caregivers Marketplace (www.caregiversmarketplace.com), offering rebates on Huggies diapers (among a few hundred other products). This rebate program is unique in its broad range of products, number of submissions allowed (more than one per household), and the length of the offers (ours was good for a full year). We were able to earn $1 back on each pack of diapers we bought for nearly two years. That was one we were sure to take full advantage of!

> $ **Centsable Tip** $
>
> Most rebate programs will give you a full rebate even if you use a coupon. Whenever we bought Huggies diapers we always used a coupon and sent in for the rebate to get double the savings!

Sales Cycle Shopping

The last incentive that spans across several stores is *sales cycle shopping*. Sales cycles are simply a pattern of when specific loss leaders appear, which may be in any given month of the year. We have been able to save significant money on both grocery and home goods just by being aware of sales cycles. Some sales cycles make perfect sense while others just exist and we don't know why. Last year we were able to pick up five-pound bags of brand-name whole wheat flour on sale for $1.68, though it typically sells for about $3.00 a bag. Because we knew the sales cycle for baking goods is in a six-month rotation we purchased what we would need to last us until the next sales cycle. We saved almost 50% just like that on something our family uses every week.

Nearly every product falls into some sales cycle. You can find barbecue items on sale from April to July but the deepest discounts in most areas will be just before and after Memorial Day, the Fourth of July, and Labor Day (sometimes longer!). Just after Christmas you will find linens, towels, and bedding on sale (commonly known as "White Sales") and often electronics and appliances into February. March is National Frozen Foods month (who knew?), and just before Thanksgiving and Christmas you can find bargains on baking goods.

This is a simple way to shop without using coupons that can still save you a bunch.

Action Plan

1. Contact your local stores to ask about incentive programs.
   a. Some questions you will want to ask include:
      i. Do you accept manufacturer coupons? Do you accept Internet (printable) coupons? Are there any value restrictions (for example, no coupons over $1)?
      ii. Do you price-match? If so, what specific stores or within what radius? Are there restrictions on the offers you will match?
      iii. Do you offer specials requiring a loyalty or member card? Where and how can I get one?
      iv. Do you have any special shopper incentive programs? Where can I find the details about these programs?

    v. Do you double coupons? What are the restrictions (on value and quantity)?

  b. Be sure to sign up for loyalty cards or programs at the stores you *think* you may shop at. It's better to have it already when you stop in than to have to do it at the checkout when you're in a hurry.

2. Check out BeCentsable.net for:

  a. Links to rebate programs you can take advantage of.

  b. A printable sales cycle chart for the full year.

  c. More information on drugstore incentive plans.

3

The Art of Stockpiling

Stockpiling is simply planning ahead (a theme we feel is so important, we will focus on it for the next two chapters). The advantage to stocking up is taking advantage of a great deal so we don't have to pay full price the next time we need that item. In this chapter we will explain reasons to stockpile, address storage concerns, and outline the best way to get started.

Stockpiling is like planting and tending a garden. The best gardeners are those who plant crops they will use, put in the extra time at the beginning to care for their garden, and then regularly maintain it throughout the year. Starting a great stockpile requires a little planning to ensure money and space are not wasted. A gardener would be unlikely to plant and tend crops he or she wouldn't use and, likewise, a stockpile is not helpful if money and storage space are wasted on products not being used up. As a stockpile grows, the work to maintain it is considerably less than the work required to get it started. Each week your stockpile will be running low on just one or two items. These can easily be replenished if time was invested in the beginning to get started right.

Why Stockpile?

If we were asked what single shopping strategy would save the most money, our answer would emphatically be *stockpiling*! Why? The idea behind stockpiling is to buy items when they are at their lowest price and to buy enough to last your family until the item is at its lowest price again (usually three to six months). Our families eat a lot of cereal. It's a bedtime snack, a morning meal, an easy dry food on the go . . . so when we see cereal on sale we really stock up. Recently Chrissy was able to get Kellogg's cereal for just 8¢ a box by combining a great sale with coupons. That's a price you won't see every week. Since cereal stays fresh on the shelf for months, Chrissy took advantage of the stock-up principle and saved 98% on the cost of cereal for her family!

> Of all the things I learned at my BeCentsable workshop I think stockpiling is the strategy that has saved me the most money. It took me about three months to get a good stock-pile going but once I did it helped cut my grocery budget by 25%! Every time an item our family uses regularly hits rock bottom I stock up. My kids love to eat fruit snacks, so when I was able to get fruit snacks for 25¢ a box I stocked up for three months.
>
> —*Carrie*

Stockpiling plays an important role in helping meet your budget, no matter what it is. The idea behind the BeCentsable program is not simply to spend as little as possible, it's to spend as little as possible on the things your family loves. Let's use an example from our lives to illustrate the impact stockpiling can have. We love spinach lasagna; it's healthy, it tastes good, and it's a sneaky way to get our kids to eat spinach! It's also one of our most costly meals to make. We make this meal once a month and there is never a bite that gets thrown out. If we were to buy the ingredients to make this meal at random or, worse yet, at the last minute, it would cost around $15 (depending on the region of the country you live in). By timing our purchases to get the lowest possible price and stocking up when we get that price, we are able to cut out 64% of that cost (see table below).

Spinach Lasagna

	Regular Price	Rock-Bottom Price (using sales/coupons)
Ingredients to Stockpile		
Frozen Spinach	$1.98	$.99
Lasagna Noodles	$2.00	$.50
Pasta Sauce	$2.78	$.50
Shredded Cheese	$2.99	$1.50
Ingredients That Cannot Be Stockpiled		
Ricotta Cheese	$3.98	$.99
TOTAL	$13.73	$4.48
Single Meal Savings	$9.25	
Six-Month Savings	$55.50	

The Storage Question

What we've described above is just one meal a month. Imagine the possibilities!

But, you may say (as we did), I have two dogs, two kids, a husband, and a serious shoe addiction! There's no room!

Even in the tiniest house ever built, there are ways around storage limitations. Neither of us has a large home and we both have our fair share of clutter. However, we found simple solutions to the storage concerns we had when starting this program.

When we were just starting our own stockpiles, we envisioned every nook and cranny of our homes filled with the loot from our great deals. Honestly, just the thought of it drove us a little batty. We learned a stockpile could hurt our budget if we didn't plan properly. Snagging great deals is a ton of fun (and more than a little bit addictive) but there are two very good arguments for the "less is more" approach to stockpiling. First, stocking up on every great deal you come across will leave less money for the things your family really needs, and second, your storage space (and time) are not being used most efficiently if space is wasted. Back to our garden: it wouldn't make sense to plant an acre of watermelons and be forced buy tomatoes from our neighbor when we could plant half an acre of each and still have plenty to eat. If deodorant and fifty-roll packages of toilet paper are on sale this week and storage space is limited, stock up on the deodorant. This will leave space for stocking up next week, resulting in higher savings.

The easiest way to create extra storage space is to clear out things that are no longer being used. We found tons of extra cabinet space just by going through our dishes and getting rid of things we weren't making good use of. Kristin and her husband recently cleaned out their kitchen cabinets to make room for food storage. They were amazed at what they found that they weren't using. Small appliances, dishes, silverware, old spices, and more baking dishes than one family could ever use were all taking up unnecessary space. After a little rearranging and a lot of clutter clearing, they came up with two entire cabinets that could be used for food storage. We also found additional storage space by reorganizing our linen closets and bathroom cabinets for personal care items. A great place to store dry goods is in a dry, dark garage or laundry room. We each found inexpensive shelves for these spaces (check garage sales, other resale sources, or local discount stores) and now we are able to store most of our stockpile items away from the day-to-day living spaces in our homes.

> $ **Centsable Tip** $
>
> It's important to keep stored foods dry, off the floor, and away from direct sunlight to preserve quality.

One of the most often asked questions at our workshops and by BeCentsable members is how to stock up on and store refrigerated and freezer goods. Neither of us has a deep freezer, just run-of-the-mill side-by-side refrigerator/freezers, although Kristin does have a second, smaller refrigerator/freezer in the garage for extra milk (her family really needs a cow!).

Starting Your Own Stockpile (the Right Way) Without Losing Your Mind

As we mentioned, to be beneficial, stockpiling should be an intentional act, not part of an impulse trip to the grocery store. It is easy to become overwhelmed with the magnitude of the potential for stocking up, to end up with a fabulous stockpile but have nothing to make dinner with, or to lose momentum. All that is needed to combat these challenges is a plan. Many shoppers simply don't know where to start. Below we will outline how to get started on your own stockpile, the right way. Your stockpile won't appear overnight, but be steadfast: the financial benefits are worth it.

Before we take the first step, we should mention that we do have one general budgeting tip that we used, and we pass it on to our workshop attendees. When we went out shopping for items on our stock-up list it was hard to decide how many items to focus on each week. Plan on using 25% of each week's budget toward stock-up items. This should leave enough room in your budget to get all of the things you would have purchased before. This works because you are now saving an extra 25% by shopping smart even for items not at rock bottom.

1. Begin by stockpiling coupons.

    We talked in detail about coupons in chapter 1. It's simple to collect multiple coupons for a product your family uses regularly. We usually buy two or three newspapers each weekend or order coupons or inserts from a coupon clipping service. It will take about four weeks of regularly collecting extra coupon inserts to begin using them to get rock-bottom deals.

2. Create storage space based on your family's needs (refer back to the section on storage).

3. Create your family's focus item list.

    Creating a focus item list helps keep your purchases in line with your family's needs. Simply fill out the form, available for download on our website, with the most costly items in your budget each month or the items you buy most often. Stocking up on these focus items can help eliminate time-wasting last-minute trips to the store and save money. Chrissy's family uses a lot of shredded cheese. Shredded cheese happens to be one of the more expensive dairy products and there are seldom coupon offers available. But when shredded cheese is on sale Chrissy can buy (and freeze) enough to last her family for three months. She buys enough for three months because she knows that shredded cheese is on sale at her rock-bottom price of less than $1.50 a bag about once every twelve weeks. She saves $24 every three months just by buying shredded cheese at the right time. This takes no more time at the store than buying one package of cheese. An important part of this exercise is noting which of the focus items can be stocked up on. This helps to stay focused at the store.

The table on the opposite page is an example of Kristin's focus item list and her savings potential.

4. Begin paying closer attention to prices and sales cycles.

It's important to know what the rock-bottom price is in your area for a specific item on your stock-up list. This number will not always be the same—it's relative to the current best price you know you can find (or have found in the past). For example, if cereal is regularly priced at $2.50 a box, the rock-bottom price is something less than $2.50, hopefully about 50% less, around $1.25 per box. This is the price at which we recommend stocking up with enough to last your family three to six months. Ideally, the stock-up time for each item will follow a regular sales cycle. We discussed sales cycles in chapter 2.

5. Use the stockable items from your focus item list to start your stockpile.

Look through the weekly grocery ads and pick out the stock-up items for your shopping trip each week. Limit yourself to one or two items each week when you start. Stay focused on only items your family uses already (or is willing to substitute).

Focus Item	Regular Price	Rock-Bottom Price	Quantity for Six Months	Savings for Six Months
Cereal	$3.62	$.50	36	$112.32
Yogurt (24 oz.)	$3.29	$1.99	36	$46.80
Milk (gal.)	$3.64	$1.47	108	$234.36
Bread (1.5-lb. loaf)	$2.99	$1.82	18	$21.06
Frozen Heat-and-Eat Meals	$3.13	$2.00	48	$54.24
TOTALS	$16.67	$7.78		$468.78
Savings on a Single Purchase	$8.89			

Many more foods can be frozen than most shoppers think. Do a little research to find out what products in your family's diet can be frozen.

$ **Centsable Tip** $

A lot of dairy products can be frozen and still maintain their quality, taste, and texture. For example, if there is a great deal on milk, we will purchase extra and freeze it. This is especially helpful when you have little ones drinking different milk from what the rest of the family drinks and at a much slower pace. When our girls were younger, we were constantly at the store buying half gallons or pints of whole milk to try to keep a fresh supply. Then we discovered we could freeze it. Good-bye to dragging two grumpy children to the grocery store twice a week for milk! We simply pour an inch or two off the top (this is an important step, because the frozen milk will expand inside the container), recap, and place upright in the freezer. Other dairy products, such as yogurt and shredded and sliced cheese, can be frozen as well.

6. Stock up on ingredients for "family favorites."

Each family has a rotating menu of meals that are considered favorites, probably five to ten, depending on how often meals are eaten away from home each week. These are meals that are easy to make because the recipe has been committed to memory and everyone usually eats without complaint. Many families don't even realize they have these meals. We didn't! After stocking up on focus items, a list of stockable items from your family favorites list will become your new stock-up guide. We demonstrated earlier how stocking up on the ingredients for just one meal a month can save big. Imagine multiplying that by five or ten!

Spend a few minutes thinking about the meals your family has eaten over the past few weeks. Write down the ones that could be considered family favorites. Next, list the ingredients for each recipe and make a note of the ones that are stockable. This is the next round of stock-up items to focus on.

I can't believe how easy it was to make my stockpile list. I made a list of my focus items and our favorite meals, then I just took all the items on the two lists that were stockable to create my new stockpile list! This list helps to ensure that I didn't stock up on unnecessary items and waste money.

—*Angela*

Action Plan

1. Continue collecting and filing coupons each week (read more about this in chapter 1).
2. Make a focus item list.

3. Make a list of "family favorites" meals.
4. Visit BeCentsable.net for links to the resources and forms referenced in this chapter.
    a. Forms:
        i. Family favorite meals form.
        ii. Stock-up guide and pantry list.
    b. Resources and references:
        i. Coupon insert schedule.
        ii. Sales cycle listing.

4

Planning, Planning, Planning, and Planning to Plan

Why Are We Still Talking About This?

If there is one thing we have learned from the journey we've taken together over the past two and a half years, it's that planning is the key to everyone's success. If we do a great job collecting coupons, and even snag some amazing deals at the store, but never take the time to plan, we will still be failing at being centsable because we are not using our savings efficiently. We may even be spending money to make up for our lack of organization by making last-minute trips to the store to pick up one or two items for dinner that we forgot to buy over the weekend, or by wasting foods whose purpose in our pantry wasn't clearly defined.

In all the workshops and conversations we've had on the topic of saving money, the most commonly voiced concern is the lack of planning or lack of knowledge about planning. Either shoppers find the planning process too complicated, and seemingly not useful, or they aren't sure where to begin. We will share with you what we've learned and what works for us and the hundreds of other shoppers we've had the opportunity to talk to.

What Was Planning Like for Us Before BeCentsable?

Our idea of "planning" used to consist of making a mental list while driving to the store each week. "I think we should have meat loaf this week, stuffed shells, and homemade pizza." As we meandered through the store we would compare our mental meal plan with our mental pantry list. In the end we'd arrive home with everything, unload, and get ready to start dinner only to find we bought the bread crumbs we already had and skipped the ground turkey, a key ingredient in our "plans." Now we are left with only three options: scratch the carefully made dinner plans for something else we have on hand, go out to eat, or head back to the store. Other weeks we wouldn't even bother with the mental lists; instead, we would browse the aisles looking for something that sounded good, and then try to remember the recipe and either end up buying three things we already had at home or missing the ground turkey again!

$ **Centsable Tip** $

Do not go to the store with a mental list; it is impossible to make a menu plan, create a shopping list for it, and remember everything on it when you need to, all in your head!

Not only were we missing out on savings by not knowing (or caring) what was on sale or in season, we were buying much of our food without a useful purpose. Even if there was a purpose in our head for it, it would often be lost between the store and home and the item might sit on the pantry shelves for weeks or months before being found again.

This lack of organization in your kitchen will become a vicious cycle of forgotten items and random trips to the store several times a week, where "just a quick trip for sour cream" turns into four bags of stuff you still don't have a plan for. We've all been there, done that.

Don't Repeat Our Mistake

Don't ever go (or send someone else) to the store for just one item. It's impossible to leave a grocery store without other products sneakily finding their way into the basket!

Why We Didn't Plan

It's not that we didn't want to be organized and efficient; it's not that we didn't want to save money . . . we simply had a roadblock, two of them actually. First, we were unaware that we were spending so much more than we ought to be. The time it took to plan seemed wasted, in our minds, compared to the benefit we saw from it. We didn't have a clear picture of what we were spending and how much we could be saving. Second, we had no idea how to approach the planning process in a way that made sense for us. We have small children, and finding time to sit down and plan a menu, write a shopping list, and clip coupons seemed like a far-out-of-reach luxury. We honestly felt lucky even to make it to the store some weeks.

But once again, we were wrong (and, again, our husbands are enjoying this admission). Planning saves so much more than a few minutes at the store. Planning is the key step everyone needs to take in order to be successful at saving on groceries.

How We Changed Our Behavior

So, how did we go about changing our budget-draining behavior? Just as we changed how we thought about couponing, we changed our way of thinking about the benefits of planning. All of these activities should be thought of in terms of earning money rather than saving it. If thirty minutes of planning time saves $50, we've really earned $50! If we aren't taking the time to plan we will be spending the additional money. How many part-time jobs pay $50 for a half hour of work, tax free, from the comfort of home?

With time and practice, most shoppers will become more efficient planners, but at first, don't be surprised if it takes longer than expected. Being familiar with prices and sales cycles, having a good collection of coupons, and knowing your family's menu style make this activity much easier but take some time to learn.

The really great thing about time spent planning is that it reduces time spent shopping. We used to spend a lot of time in the store aimlessly shopping with our mental lists, trying to remember everything. We may spend twice as much time planning our menus and shopping trips as we used to, but we are now getting in and out of the store in a snap and we don't have two or three trips back throughout the week for forgotten items that end up filling our baskets with $100 worth of other stuff. That's time and money saved—oops, *earned*! This extra time spent planning can be done at home, even in our pajamas. Much more relaxing than listening to our children bicker or cry because they've been stuck in a shopping cart for an hour while we try to remember if there is any cheese at home for snacks this week.

Once the rewards of planning are seen and felt, it's easy to do it every week. Recently Chrissy spent two hours planning and shopping on one of her larger grocery trips. She was able to save $187.88.

That's over $93 an hour she earned by being a centsable, organized shopper. Chrissy certainly didn't make that much when she was teaching!

Don't Repeat Our Mistake

When we were first learning and researching our program, we wasted too much time comparing ourselves to other, more frugal shoppers spending $30 or $40 a week on groceries. What were we doing wrong? It took a while, but we realized that our families were so different there was no way we could achieve the same budget without making sacrifices and dietary changes we were either not able or not willing to make. Success for us now is simply saving more than we used to. It takes time to build up a stockpile and a good collection of coupons. The point of our program is to save on the things your family wants . . . not to revamp your lifestyle to spend less than other shoppers.

Now we will walk you through the steps to start planning to earn money, not just save money!

How Often to Plan and Shop

The frequency of planning sessions will be directly dependent on the frequency of your shopping trips. There is no right or wrong way to approach this. The decision is mostly a personal choice and partly a logistical one. For example, free time for planning, payday frequency, work or school schedules, and proximity to stores with the best deals would all be factors to consider. There are several different options and pros and cons to each that most shoppers haven't even realized, let alone considered. These are outlined below to help in your decision making.

Shop once a week and avoid "dropping in" at the grocery or drugstore.

We recommend this schedule for beginners, those building a stockpile or shopping on a tight budget. Shopping weekly ensures that you can take advantage of all sales and allows you to purchase only a small amount of food at a time. This is also good for families with less storage space. The only disadvantage is there must be time to plan every week.

This is the approach we started with. It was relatively easy for us to "learn the ropes" when we were at the stores every week seeing prices, noting sales, and practicing strategies. We were also able to plan menus for one week at a time without pressure. We'll talk in more detail about menu planning in the next section.

Shop every ten days and allow for occasional stops for perishables such as milk and produce.

This is a great option for families whose schedules are a little busier. Shopping once every ten days, it is still possible to hit all the sales at the grocery stores and build a great stockpile. Nearly every grocery store runs sale ads for seven days at a time. It is easy to catch both the tail end of one sales period and the beginning of the next using this approach. Only three additional days are being added to the menu plan. On the downside, it is much more difficult to stretch perishables for ten days. It is possible to work around this by purchasing canned and frozen fruits and vegetables and checking to find the milk with an expiration date furthest out. However, an in-between run to the grocery store may be necessary in this case. Just take care that your shopping basket doesn't end up full of items that weren't on your list.

Chrissy often shops every ten days due to her family's busy schedule over the spring and fall months. Her husband is a high school coach and during these seasons he often works long hours and is gone on the weekend for team activities. During these months Chrissy has no choice but to take her two young children with her if she's going to the store. This schedule allows her to spend less time in the store each week and still take advantage of each week's specials.

Shop one time each month and assume it will be necessary to stop two or three additional times a month for perishables.

If your family's schedule is very busy, one big shopping trip every month, with smaller ones in between for produce and other perishables, is perfectly acceptable. This approach is great for times when schedules are just too hectic to plan and shop weekly or even every other week. We recommend shoppers only use this method once a basic stockpile is in place and menu planning is getting easier. This method also works well for wholesale club shoppers, as buying in bulk, especially meat, can save money and help stretch out your visits to the store. Be sure to divide, label, and freeze bulk meats right away for use later in the month. The obvious downside to this is that it allows you to take advantage of only one week of sales and specials. Starting a stockpile with this shopping schedule will add a considerable length of time to see measurable savings.

Recently Kristin used this shopping approach. She did not want to have to be shopping while her family was visiting, so she opted for a big shopping trip over a holiday weekend. She was able to get everything she needed for her family and her guests and still save a lot of money, over 50%. The key to this was her already extensive stockpile and taking advantage of a holiday weekend sale to get some phenomenal prices.

Whatever approach fits your family's needs is the best one for you. Remember that you can switch back and forth between methods, as each of us does, to meet changing demands on your schedule. The goal is to organize your trips to earn money and have a purpose for everything that goes into the shopping basket.

The last aspect of an actual shopping trip to consider is which day of the week you will do your shopping. Believe it or not, there may be a "better" day to shop! Grocery store sale ads typically run from midweek to midweek, starting Wednesday and ending on the following Tuesday, with a few running Sunday to Saturday. National retailers run ads Sunday through Saturday. Special holiday sales and promotions are usually offered on Mondays and Fridays. What does all of this mean? Most important, unless there has been ample time in your schedule to review the brand-new sales flyer and clip coupons, try to avoid shopping on the first day of a sale. Quite often, at drug- and national retail stores, the really great deals will be gone right away: the day or two after sales ads come out. Grocery stores tend to run low on loss leaders on Mondays after the weekend rush.

It's good to find out when your local stores restock (Tuesday evening or early Wednesday morning, for example) and time your shopping trip around this information if you have the option.

The Planning Process

We've broken planning into five steps to help maintain focus and save time. These five steps are always the same.

1. Look for rock-bottom deals.
2. Pick which items to stock up on.
3. Plan your menu from the sales ad.
4. List what you are planning to buy and at which stores.
5. Clip coupons for the items on your list.

Making lists and coordinating a grocery trip seemed to us like an attempt to make the stars align. Little did we know, if the five steps above are followed, the stars actually do align!

> Before I attended a BeCentsable workshop I had no idea I was wasting so much money by not planning. Now I spend more time at home planning but less time at the store. Once I started making a list and only buying what was on the list, I saw that I was spending considerably less! At least 25% less, maybe more!
>
> —Mary

First, We Look for Rock-Bottom Deals

The first, most basic step is simply to look through the sales ads for loss leaders: items that are discounted greatly to get shoppers in the door. Pick the ones your family uses and that fit in your budget for the week (or month). Remember, we aim to use about 25% of our household goods budget to build a stockpile. This step took us the longest at the beginning when we were less familiar with "regular" prices. We used to spend hours looking over the ads and calling each other. For example, was $1.99 per pound for grapes a great deal? Was $3.49 per pound for ground beef reasonable? We didn't have a clue in the beginning. We were also disappointed to learn that the sales flyers were not just promoting products the stores had on sale; we learned from a recent *Consumer Reports* study that they were also promoting products whose brand or distributor was paying to have them placed on a specific page, even if the price was not reduced.[1] We had to learn the prices just so we would know if we were looking at true sales or if we were simply seeing a "phantom sale," which is the same as an advertisement. This knowledge base is acquired over time with consistent exposure, and while it is important to have, it is also nice to have someone else do the work for us. Our website was created, in part, for this very purpose.

We struggled to find a way to make this first, important task simpler and faster. After searching without luck for the help we needed, we decided to create the solution rather than hoping someone else would do it. We gathered a community of bloggers who were already being centsable and were willing to share their knowledge and we asked them to participate in our new community. Now the best resources are gathered on our site for shoppers who know their local stores inside and out to share with the rest of us what's really a great deal and what's just a paid advertisement. As if that alone wasn't helpful enough, these shoppers also offer coupon match-ups for us; that's simply a quick notation (refer to chapter 1

1   http://www.mainstreet.com/article/smart-spending/budgeting/consumer-reports-13-tips-save-groceries?page=2.

for a detailed example of these notations) to help shoppers quickly find and clip relevant coupons to use in conjunction with the sale. It's important to still look over the grocery ads for other items your family may need that are not at rock-bottom prices.

> I love the resources I can find at BeCentsable.net! They help me find the best deals without spending so much time looking through the ads. It's nice to have all of that information available in one place. I really like that the coupons are already noted for me—what a time saver! Thanks to all the hardworking shoppers out there who share their knowledge with the rest of us!
>
> —*Kara*

Despite hundreds of resources available (you can find them all on our website), there are cases where a quick and easy solution just isn't available. Some shoppers still prefer to do the legwork themselves. In this case there are some tips and advice we can offer to make the task a little less daunting. The most difficult part will be identifying the best deals. It takes time but putting intentional thought into this will help it stick in your memory. Remember to balance time spent looking over the ads with time spent making a menu and gathering coupons. It may be helpful to set a timer for twenty or thirty minutes the first few times. Step away and come back later if the activity is proving difficult. It's okay to move ahead to some minor menu planning (we'll get into more detail in the next section) and come back to this part.

Choose Which of the Great Deals to Stockpile

After browsing the ads and looking online, we must now decide which of the rock-bottom deals our family is going to pick up this week. Even if there are ten really great deals we'd like to stock up on, chances are we don't have that much storage space or room in our budget. We choose the deals that are the most helpful to our pocketbook and will fit in the space available. Again, this is a balance between saving money and keeping life simple.

Menu Planning Made Simple

We've said it before, we'll say it again . . . items purchased without a clear purpose will be forgotten about or lost in the pantry! This is wasted money. Now, we're obviously not saying a random great deal must be avoided if it's not part of the current week's plan. We're saying when a product breaks the smart shopper force field around your cart, it only does so because it has a distinct purpose in your kitchen.

Also, a menu plan is not meant to become a way to identify what day of the week it is: Taco Tuesday, Meat Loaf Friday, Spaghetti Sunday. Oh, we can hear the groans now! No, no, menu planning is meant to create flexibility—meal options for your family without stress, without last-minute trips to the store for that missing final ingredient. We will help you create an easy system that will flex with your family's needs and save money.

This is the most important meal-planning tip we can offer you: plan your meals around the sales ads. That's it, simple, completely logical, yet we discover half the shoppers we talk to are not doing this. We were dumbfounded at our own ignorance the first time someone suggested this approach to us. It's so simple. . . . Just look at the sale ad first and see what is on sale or in season and plan your menu around these items. For example, Chrissy sees that rice, zucchini, and peppers are on sale this week. This is a perfect week for her to make stir-fry. In the past we simply cooked what sounded good without considering what was in season or on sale. As a consequence, some meals ended up costing us three or four times what they should have. We were making special purchases to cook our menu and nearly always paying full price for each individual ingredient. Don't feel bad if you've not been planning your meals around the sales ads; apparently it's an elusive concept! Refer back to our idea of "planning" for a moment; don't repeat our mistake.

The first step to menu planning is, as always, to get organized. We typically give our pantries, stockpile. and freezer a quick scan so we know what's available for menu planning. Set aside some time to organize your family's favorite recipes to make meal planning simpler. Remember that meal planning doesn't mean every meal must be planned. It simply means: plan something. Some families are too busy to plan a meal for every night of the week. Create the meal plan that works for your family with the triple goal of making dinners healthier, stress-free, and less expensive. Even if the meal for the night is "clean out the fridge," if it's on the menu plan, the work of remembering is already done!

A few general meal-planning tips are important to put to use no matter how we actually find and choose meals. First, we try to use sale items for more than one recipe for the week. For example, if ground beef is on sale, our meal plan might include chili, tacos, and meat loaf. This also allows us to do a small bit of bulk cooking, the "cook once, eat twice" approach. Chrissy's family does this when ground turkey is on sale. She stocks up and will often make a meat loaf and meatballs in the same day, then freeze one for a meal later in the week or month. This saves time and money. Second, it's important to balance the cost of meals in your meal plan. We outline a method of tracking this within your own recipe collection below. We try to keep most of our meals to $5–$7 each. If one night we are having an unusually expensive meal (steaks or salmon fillets) we will try to balance that with a less expensive meal another night that week. Finally, we always make sure to write down our meal plan. Some weeks we want to be ultraorganized and plan out every day; other weeks, we just make a list of the meals we could cook and pick one from the list each day. We don't want to forget what we intended to do with that bag of spinach we got for free!

There are several different methods for menu planning and we've tried them all, ranging from a traditional do-it-yourself style to having someone else assign a meal plan to us each week. There are benefits to each one. Take your pick! We explain the options in more detail below.

The most common approach is to simply do it yourself.

YOU WILL NEED:

- Three-ring binder, or large recipe box
- Tab dividers for option selected above
- Highlighter, pen, or marker
- Copies of your "family favorites" recipes

WHAT TO DO:

1. Gather your family's favorite recipes. Write them on index cards, photocopy the originals, or print them from the computer.
2. Look through each recipe in detail and mark the items that could be included in your stockpile.
3. Label the dividers by main ingredient (e.g., chicken, beef, fish, poultry, pork, vegetable, fruit).
4. Organize the recipes in the same manner and place them in the binder (a separate color highlighter may be helpful to make the main ingredient easy to find on the page or card).

5. An optional but very helpful step: include a ranking of the expense of the meal at the top right corner of the recipe page or card and sort within each category by these numbers.

1 = least expensive ($0–$5 meal)—chili, tacos, tuna casserole, leftovers, baked potato bar

2 = more expensive ($6–$10 meal)—breaded chicken strips, homemade veggie pizza, grilled pork loin

3 = most expensive ($11+ meal)—lasagna, grilled salmon, shrimp fettuccine, steaks

A good mixture of recipes from each of these meal price categories will help keep your budget in check and provide a good variety. Remember, this step is not necessary, just helpful. If this is too much detail, tailor a recipe retrieval and management system that will work for you.

It's also nice to have a little help to spice up your menu plan.
Several dozen tools are available to make menu planning easier by offering searchable recipe databases and customized shopping lists, even storing favorite family recipes and making them searchable by ingredients.

Online tools and resources are especially helpful for finding recipes with ingredients already on hand or on your shopping list at rock-bottom prices. Most of the recipe databases and programs will also make a grocery list based on selected recipes. Recipe databases tend to be user created and allow the community to rate and comment on each recipe, which is very helpful.

Software programs are varied and offer a wide-ranging set of functions. Entire cookbooks can be included in some of the programs as well as family recipes. The programs can be set up to filter recipes by ingredient, nutritional content, or dietary restriction; to offer substitution suggestions or cut or increase yield; and to make a menu plan and even a grocery list that's organized by aisle! The cost is $50–$100 for the base copy of the software and $20–$30 for additional cookbook downloads. These programs are definitely an investment but if used properly, they are well worth the money. Kristin's children are both on a gluten-free diet and the program's ability to filter out gluten-containing foods in recipes and offer substitutions is a huge time saver for her. We both also use AllRecipes.com a great deal to find recipes by specific ingredient.

More helpful still, let someone else do the legwork!

Some companies offer full weekly menu plans based on sales cycles at national and select regional grocery store chains. These meal plans are created for two to four family members, with options for several different diets (e.g., low fat or low carb) and made available on a weekly basis. Subscriptions to these services cost between $5 and $30 a month.

The downside to these services is the restricted options for the week; however, having a menu plan handed to us is such a time saver on busy weeks that we think it's worth it once in a while.

Rock-bottom deals? Done! Menu plan? Done!

Refining Our Shopping List and Choosing Which Stores to Visit

Now it's time to make our actual shopping list. We may have some notes of things we've seen in the ads or thought of throughout the process but now we are going to refine the list. First we note the rock-bottom deals we want to take advantage of and the store where we can find them (we often write down the ad price as well so we don't have to go back to the ad again later). We then note any additional items we need to execute our meal plan for the week. We often evaluate these items closely before actually placing them on the list. Do we have to have grated vanilla bean or can we get by with vanilla extract? In other words, we try to find substitutes for specialty items to avoid costly one-time purchases and we will sometimes swap out basic ingredients for things we already have on hand. For example, gluten-free pasta is rather expensive. If Kristin has a pasta dish on her menu for the week, she may decide to make that dish with rice she already has in her pantry, a much cheaper alternative to the pasta. Last, we add items to the list that are likely the catalyst for the trip in the beginning. This final group of items is made up of those things we cannot do without: milk, produce, cheese (for Kristin it always includes coffee), dog food, diapers—whatever our family is out of that is pushing us to go today or very soon!

Once our full shopping list is complete, we need to spend a few minutes reevaluating to choose the stores we plan to visit. We may have selected deals from more than four stores and end up only visiting two or decide to visit all four. We don't need to catch every great deal as long as we are focusing on items that will have the biggest impact in our budget. Of all the factors to consider, the most important is making sure we stock up on our family's focus items and the ingredients for family favorite meals. The great thing about this plan is it's up to us!

Don't Repeat Our Mistake

It's easy to get sidetracked by the idea of snagging a great deal and forget about what getting it could cost. When we were first starting out, we made the mistake of driving twenty minutes to a local store to take advantage of a "great deal" that actually cost us more in gas than we saved on the items we purchased.

Some questions we typically ask ourselves:

1. How great are the deals this week?
   - If they are just so-so, skip a few, get the one or two best "can't pass it up" deals, and save yourself some time.
   - Accounting for gas and time required to get from store to store is important.
2. Can I get it at another store?
   - Sometimes the loss leaders are very close in price from store to store.
   - Manufacturers' promotions are often nationwide and deals on in-season produce will probably show up at several stores in a region.
   - If this is the case, consider consolidating these items from several stores into one even if there are a few pennies' difference in price. In the end, the time versus money equation will balance out.
3. How much time is really available?
   - Be realistic. It's not worth the stress to try to squeeze three stops into a forty-five-minute allotment (unless it's possible to do it without feeling rushed or speeding from store to store—a speeding ticket will probably eat up all your savings!).
4. Is there an alternative?
   - For example, we both participate in co-ops in our area so we seldom make a special stop for produce deals.
   - We also price-match when we have busy weeks or just don't feel like visiting multiple stores.
   - Use your friends! Chrissy used to pick up a few items for Kristin on her trips when there was a really great deal. Kristin would return the favor. This saves time and gas.

When first getting started, we recommend shoppers visit at least two stores each week, one local grocery store and one drugstore. This helps to boost savings and speeds stockpiling. Once your stockpile is in place, a once-a-month trip to the drugstore should be sufficient to maintain it. Remember that this plan is supposed to work for your family. Don't drive yourself crazy visiting four stores every week just to save a few extra dollars. We encourage families to find the right balance between saving time and saving money!

Last Step—Find and Clip Coupons

The last task in our five-step system is to search for and clip the coupons we will be using on the shopping trip we've carefully planned. This step will reinforce why the coupon filing system we recommend is so wonderful! Refer to chapter 1 for details of this system and to see the reference codes.

We may already have some coupons noted on our list from our Internet research but we need to take a few minutes to search for coupons for the rest of the items we plan to buy. All we need for this activity is our computer and a pen. We look up each and every item in one of the free online coupon databases.

Usually a brand-name search will be all we need to do, but sometimes a product category search will retrieve a great coupon we weren't able to find the other way. When we find a coupon we want to clip, we write down the reference information (e.g., 6/21 SS) next to the item on our grocery list. If we find a printable coupon, we simply print it out right then and set it aside for clipping. After searching the coupon databases, we may visit company websites for items on our list we have not yet found coupons for. These will either be printable coupons or coupons we can request by mail. Obviously, printable coupons are what we'll be searching for, but the direct-mail offers are great to take advantage of for a later trip.

The final step is to clip the coupons we plan to use. This is something we often do the day of our shopping trip (sometimes just as we are walking out the door). It doesn't take long to do this, probably five or ten minutes. We usually take our coupon file box, our portable coupon organizer, a pair of scissors, and our grocery list to the kitchen table for this project. Our coupon inserts are filed in date order so we simply go down our grocery list and pull out the corresponding insert, flip through to find the coupon we've noted on our grocery list, and clip it out.

We put all of our coupons in the appropriate pocket of our small portable organizer, grab a calculator and a pen, and put everything in a reusable shopping bag for our trip to the store!

How much time will all of this take? Is it really worth it?

An obvious question most shoppers ask at this point is "How long does all of this take?" The process sounds involved and lengthy at first. And while our system does take more time than most shoppers currently spend, this actually usually takes far less time than you might expect.

Actually, when we combined our planning time and compared it to the time we used to spend in the store shopping—both the initial trip and returning a few times a week for the inevitable forgotten item—we found we were actually saving time along with money! Even if we did spend the same amount of time as before, when we consider that we are also usually saving somewhere around 50% of our total grocery bill, the benefit is undeniable. Our time on this process each week is worth hundreds to our family over the course of a month; thousands over a year. For Chrissy's family, the thousands they are saving and applying to their mortgage is increased by the interest they are also cutting. For Kristin's family, the extra money recently allowed them to purchase a new vehicle with cash, a savings again improved further by cutting out loan interest.

Action Plan

1. Plan for this week's shopping trip.
   a. Look for rock-bottom deals.
      i. Get familiar with sales ads and rock-bottom deals and pick out items for your stockpile.
         (1) Practice finding the deals.
         (2) Use resources available at BeCentsable.net to make this process easier!
   b. Pick which deals to stockpile.
   c. Plan your menu.
      i. Organize your recipes.
         (1) Use a file box or binder, *and/or*:
         (2) Consider using an online recipe database or computer software to help make the process easier, or subscribe to a meal-planning service.
   d. Make a shopping list and choose which stores to visit.
      i. Remember to look for coupons for items on your "must-have" list in the online coupon databases found on our website.
   e. Find and clip coupons.
2. Visit BeCentsable.net for:
   a. Our grocery resources link. We promise it will save time!
   b. Links and reviews of several recipe databases and companies offering menu-planning software.
   c. Links to menu-planning services we have tried and recommend.
   d. Links to the coupon databases we have found most helpful.

5

Shopping Tips and Tricks

Shopping can be time-consuming, stressful, and expensive if you do not have a plan. We've shopped under all variety of circumstances, from driving to the store at nine p.m. to shop for the week after we realized we had absolutely nothing to cook for breakfast the next morning to visiting the store on a meticulously planned shopping trip with a menu plan waiting on the counter and a coupon for nearly everything on our list. We've shopped alone in the wee hours of the morning; we've shopped on vacation and with all four of our kids throwing temper tantrums in each aisle of the store. We've visited five stores in one day, and we've paid more for things than we should because we knew we couldn't possibly go to two stores in a week. Through it all we've finally learned what works for our family and what doesn't.

We will share with you what we've learned and help you apply it to your life to make shopping quick, easy, manageable, and affordable no matter what the circumstances.

Shopping with the Enemy

While we feel like we ought to be able to manage our children in nearly every daily activity we need to do, we've come to accept the fact that shopping (centsably) is just not one of them. It always sounds nice to have our husbands or friends tag along, to help or converse with, and they can be helpful if they understand and support what we are trying to do; some days are better than others!

Unless you are certain your spouse or friend can act as an "accountability partner"—someone who helps you focus on saving money and being smart—we always recommend shopping alone. We used to shop together frequently because we had the same goals and it was always helpful to have someone there to control our impulses. Sometimes one of us was more committed to the task than the other. On a shopping trip just before Christmas one year, Kristin was having a great time picking up all the cute stuff on sale at Target. As a result, Chrissy spent half the trip trailing behind her, asking, "Do you really need that?"

One trip in particular proved to Chrissy how much time and money could be misspent by picking the wrong time of day and the wrong shopping partner. This particular week, Chrissy thought it would be great to take advantage of being out of the house on Sunday after church to run one simple errand: a small, quick trip to the grocery store. She had about eight items on her list and was completely organized and her husband was there to help with their children. This should be a breeze! she thought. The first stop, in aisle 1, was for yogurt, and Chrissy's husband spent ten minutes picking out the flavors he wanted. On to aisle 3, where their progress was interrupted by a quick break for a diaper change. In aisle 6, Chrissy and her husband spent five minutes picking up spilled Goldfish crackers. And finally, in aisle 9, they threw in the towel when their two-year-old had a complete meltdown because there were no more crackers. What would have taken Chrissy ten or fifteen minutes alone ended up taking forty minutes, a lot of patience, and extra money on the five other items her husband found.

While we emphatically proclaim shopping alone is the best choice, we realize it's just not possible for some families—or ourselves! We often have to take our children with us. The best thing to do, next to planning our trip, is to be prepared. First and foremost, we select the time of day carefully. Kristin knows her children are not going to be happy stuck in a cart at the store anytime after eleven in the morning. She plans her trips with them for early mornings just after breakfast and allots, at most, one hour from start to finish. She has learned the hard way that it's easier on everyone to work with the family's needs rather than attempt a quick, forceful run through the store. Kristin's daughter once made it loud and clear that she did not want to be in the grocery store by tearing open a box of rice and dumping it on the floor, then she proceeded to clear the shelves while Mom was cleaning up the mess! It was rather difficult to focus on prices, lists, and coupons with one child crying in her ear and the other running from aisle to aisle saying, "Nana-nana-boo-boo, you can't catch me"! That one afternoon in the store with two unhappy little people was all it took!

> When I first started shopping on the BeCentsable plan I found that it worked best to make sure I went shopping when my husband or Grandma could watch the kids. This allowed me to focus on saving money and learning the ropes.
>
> —Kathy

Second, we are always sure to have drinks and snacks with us. Even if we've just eaten a meal, the sights and smells of the grocery store create empty bellies, lots of "I wants," and whining. Sometimes we will even make a special afternoon out of the shopping trip by eating at the deli just before shopping. Third, we try to involve our children in the shopping process when we can. As our kids get older, the grocery store becomes a great learning experience. We can engage them in a family activity, a math lesson, a personal finance lesson, and a science and nutrition lesson as well as teach the importance of family responsibilities. They can help us pick items off the shelf and put them in the cart, mark off the list, examine and sort coupons, even compare prices with a calculator.

Arm Yourself!

What we take to the store and how we keep ourselves organized in the store are key to helping us execute all the great deals we spend time planning each week. We make sure our coupons are clipped and the ones we plan to use at the store are selected and separated from others. We always have a pen, a calculator, our store loyalty cards, and the current week's ads. As we pick items up to purchase, we like to use our calculators to compare prices and even break prices into unit cost to see which brand or size is truly a better deal. When we plan our trips we estimate prices and keep ourselves within a budget. Sometimes we even like to challenge ourselves to beat our own budget for the week. We track our total to see how we are doing against our estimate.

We also bring along a coupon organizer with coupons for items we know we'd easily buy if we happened upon an unadvertised sale or clearance. These are usually items our family uses a lot of and that we can always add to our stockpiles. The organizer is small enough to fit in our purse but holds all of our shopping essentials and the extra "just in case" coupons. Because there is not a lot in the organizer, we have a sort of mental picture and seldom have to flip through it.

Outsmart the Stores

Once we are at the store there are millions of dollars' worth of research and consumer studies working against our willpower and organization to try to get us to stray from our lists and make impulse purchases. Centsable consumers can prepare themselves for battle by learning the stores' strategies. Let's sneak a peak at their playbook together!

How to Win at "Consumerism"

Marketers attract our senses first with sights, tastes, and smells in stores. The layout of many stores is specifically designed to engage shoppers and force them to enter certain areas. Even checkouts are arranged to get our one last penny out of our pocketbooks before we leave the store.

Stores spend thousands of dollars on signature scents to get us to spend more money. They strategically place the deli and bakery at the front of the store to make us hungry shoppers, and all the food samples that stores offer aren't a courtesy. They know we often shop when we are hungry and it only takes a few seconds with a product in our hands (or mouth) to convince us we need to buy it.

$ **Centsable Tip** $

Shop with a full stomach. This is the best way to combat overspending on impulse purchases. We usually write down the food samples we try and like. This gives us a chance to look for a coupon (or get a couple from the sample table to file away) and make sure the product still sounds good in a week when we aren't hungry and impressionable!

Designing strategic layouts is another way that stores engage shoppers' pocketbooks. Having made our fair share of random runs to the store to pick up "just a gallon of milk," we have had an opportunity to note that staple items like milk, produce, meat, and eggs are typically located at the back of the store. This practice is ingenious: it forces us through the aisles we wouldn't otherwise need to go down, encouraging us (or sometimes reminding us) to pick up additional items along the way.

$ **Centsable Tip** $

Avoid the in-between runs to the store for forgotten items or ingredients for that last-minute dinner plan by planning and organizing your menu and shopping trip.

Another trick stores use is product placement. According to Jack Taylor, professor of retailing at Birmingham-Southern College, manufacturers actually pay to have their products placed in certain locations on store shelves. The premium spots are those at eye level and on end caps—the short shelves at the ends, between one aisle and the next. Stores often place items on end caps to highlight sales or because a manufacturer has paid to have the item placed there. Even if the product on the end cap is truly on sale, the stores will often place tie-in items with the sale items (for example, cake mix and icing). The tie-in items are regular price but the simple fact that they're sitting on the end cap next to the sale item will encourage many consumers pick up them up rather than shop the appropriate aisle and do some price comparisons.

> $ **Centsable Tip** $
>
> When shopping each aisle, make sure to look up and down to see all the brands, sizes, and varieties available. Stay away from end caps unless the item is already on your shopping list or the item offered is an unadvertised sale or clearance, and never pick up the tie-in items. Take the extra time to look down the aisles for each item on your shopping list.

As if the placement of the product weren't enough to be wary of, the packaging and pricing of products are further avenues for undermining your careful plans. Manufacturers often have two different sizes of their better-selling products on the shelf. We tend to think the bigger package is a better bargain but that's not always the case. There are two things to consider when deciding between a smaller or a larger size. First, we use our calculator to determine if the price per unit (whatever unit of measure is on the package: ounces, pounds, each) is really lower in the larger package. In some specific products we consistently see that larger packaging is not less expensive. Surprisingly, laundry detergent and cereal are two usual culprits. Second, we think about the coupons we have and the sale (if there is one) advertised. Would we save more by buying several smaller packages with more coupons?

Don't Repeat Our Mistake

One of Kristin's big mistakes occurred when a local drugstore tricked her! Yes, we will blame it on that sneaky (but effective) marketing plan the drugstore had in place. They offered a "deal" on vinegar just after Easter. The sale offer was to buy one, get one free, for small glass bottles of white vinegar. Great for cleaning! She stocked up, only to find a jug a few weeks later with about ten times as much as the glass jars held for just a couple dollars more. Unfortunately, she had to be reminded of this goof-up for the months it took to go through all of that vinegar!

We often see items like twelve-packs of soda advertised as "buy three, get one free." This sounds terrific but we can read the fine print to see what price we will pay for each of the three we have to buy to get the fourth at no charge. Sometimes that price is 50¢ or $1 more than the price we paid at the same store the week before (they've often bumped it up to the "suggested retail price," or SRP), meaning we aren't really getting that fourth one for free—we're paying as much as $3 for it! Another common sales offer that can trick us is an offer of, say, four for $5. On that type of deal, we ask ourselves: how much is it for each one, and do we have to buy four?

Centsable Tip

We always break a sales price down to a single-unit price. If it still appears to be a good deal, we find out if the store will let us purchase just one at the discounted price. If so, we get the amount we need; if not, we only purchase the items if we can truly use that many.

Another way manufacturers can fool us is with convenience packaging. Dairy, meat, produce, and snacks are consistently offered in smaller, more convenient, on-the-go packages and we are easily fooled into grabbing these "convenience packs" thinking it's saving us some valuable amount of time. Ground beef formed into hamburger patties, chicken breasts cut into nice little strips, steaks cubed for stew—these are all conveniences but we tend to see them as commonplace. Sure, cheese sticks and preapportioned crackers, nuts, and cookies are great for those on-the-go times but we could just as easily save the extra money and spend ten minutes one day a week preparing our own snack-size portions at home! We didn't realize at first how much money we were spending on simple convenience and how much of it really didn't save that much time. For example, our children like to eat those cute little baby carrots. We dip them in hummus and ranch dressing and soft spreadable cheese. Recently we were at the store and noticed whole organic carrots were less expensive per pound than the convenient peeled (but not organic) cut baby carrots. The savings was about 50%! We can peel and cut the whole bag of carrots in about fifteen minutes. We do agree, some of the services are well worth the money. For example, skinning and deboning chicken. That's a task neither of us wants to engage in. We have to remember to ask ourselves every week at the store, how much am I willing to pay for convenience?

$ **Centsable Tip** $

Instead of thinking "This package versus that package," we try to think, "Would I pay someone to come to my home and cut these for me?" Usually the question seems ludicrous!

Stores know that when shoppers feel they are getting a good deal, they are likely to put more in their carts to sop up those perceived savings. For example, a bin of products may make us think they are a markdown or clearance item or a product that is about to expire. We often check the regular prices of the items on the shelf or try to recall what we've paid for them in the past and we always check expiration dates. This is another reason we have learned to spend most of our shopping trip in the aisles around the perimeter of the stores, where foods are marked up less (e.g., produce, meat, and dairy).

A great sales tactic stores use that we do take advantage of is marked-down dairy and meat. Late in the evening or just before closing, many stores will mark down dairy and meat they think may not sell before the "sell-by" date. Sell-by dates are not expiration dates; they are the last date at which the stores can safely sell the product for consumer preparation at home. Stores take into account the date the meat was packaged and the fact that most consumers will cook meat within two days or freeze it. In many cases, if it's an item we know we can use in the following few days or freeze right away, we'll take the great deal. We've been able to get yogurt for free and organic milk for just a dollar doing this.

Look for the following when picking up discounted meat:

1. Color and texture consistency
2. No obvious odor
3. Minimal liquid
4. Airtight wrapping

Many marked-down dairy products, such as yogurt, cheeses, sour cream, and cottage cheese, are safe to consume as long as they are purchased and used within seven days of their "use by" or "expiration" date. Yogurt specifically says this on the container; obviously we recommend using your judgment.[1]

The final stop, and the store's final chance to get our money, is the checkout. There are many strategically placed items we probably need but have forgotten, and our children are tired and the checkout line seems to be where they really start falling apart. There are cute little toys, drinks, candy, snacks. It's enough to drive even the most patient and budget-conscious shopper to the edge. When we get to the checkout we often have our older children (even toddlers and preschoolers) help by unloading the cart or putting things on the check stand. This keeps them entertained and out of trouble. Once that task is finished if they are off to create more chaos, another snack or small toy from Mom's purse might keep them busy for the few remaining minutes of the trip.

The fun is not quite over! Even at the checkout a number of things can go wrong to throw our plan out of whack. It doesn't happen often but knowing what to do to hold on to those great deals is important.

While we are shopping we often find that the store is out of stock or simply out of the size or variety we wanted for sale items that we planned to purchase. We make a note of these items on our shopping list and when we get to the checkout, we ask the cashier for a rain check. Some stores will require that we go to customer service for this. A rain check will allow us to come back the following week (sometimes longer) to pick up the items when they are back in stock, and we will pay the sale price even if the sale is no longer going. This also allows us to be sure we have

1   "A Guide to Food Expiration Dates," AssociatedContent.com (http://www
    .associatedcontent.com/article/5389/a_guide_to_food_expiration_dates
    _pg2.html?cat=22).

enough coupons for the item to really get a great deal! There are two important things to check when requesting rain checks: expiration date and quantity limits. Some stores don't list an expiration date on the rain check itself so it's important to ask. And some stores will ask how many of the product we want to purchase when we come back; they'll write that number on the rain check, and we are limited to that amount when we return. This is always a hard question for us to answer. We tend to overshoot in case we find more coupons to use.

Sometimes an item will ring up at the wrong price or a coupon will not scan. Watch the register screen as the cashier is scanning your items and your coupons. Remember, it's your money! If you think a coupon was missed or an item rang up at the wrong price, speak up! If a coupon is not scanning, it never hurts to ask the cashier to key it in manually or even to call a manager over to help. We have found that sometimes we have misread a coupon or inadvertently put the wrong item in our cart. Occasionally, we've even asked the cashier if someone can get the correct item for us while we finish our checkout. If not, at this point we may remove the item from our transaction and go back to get it later, or we may decide it's okay, we really need it and the loss of the coupon savings isn't worth a second trip through the store and checkout.

I remember when I first started how nervous I was to use coupons and store incentives. I felt that I would hold up the line or irritate the cashier. I can't believe I almost let this stop me from saving money! After using coupons and store incentives for over a year, I now realize it is my right to hold up the line for a minute to save myself money. At least once a month I have people in line ask, "How did you do that?"

or "Where did you get that great coupon?" Now I go to the register with confidence and sometimes even help people in line behind me learn a few tricks!

—Pat

As if navigating the stores, defying the marketing experts, and battling our own innate impulses weren't enough to contend with, we sometimes encounter negativity from fellow shoppers! There is nothing that can make us feel more like a nuisance than shoppers in line behind us who are quietly (or openly) impatient with the extra few minutes it takes for us to check out.

Our Mantra

It is our right to spend or save our money any way we feel is appropriate. It is our right to take advantage of the offers available to us through store sales and coupons. In the end, we are the ones working and paying for the things we need.

The final shopping strategy we practice to keep our budgets in check is paying with cash. This was a difficult transition to make at first but once we became better at planning we found that rather than feeling limited by the amount of cash we had with us at the store, we felt challenged to execute a shopping trip that included all of the things we needed within a very defined budget. As time went on, we began to feel more in control because we knew we could take a set amount of cash with us and have no trouble meeting our family's needs. We no longer hold our breath at the checkout wondering what horribly underestimated amount we spent this week!

We have experienced firsthand that practicing centsable

shopping creates diligence and a strong will to help us walk away from impulses with our money in our pockets!

Action Plan

1. Find a coupon organizer.
    a. Visit our site, BeCentsable.net, to see examples and find links to a variety of portable organizers.
    b. Be sure to include a calculator, pen, and store loyalty cards as well.
2. Learn your store's rain check policy.
3. Think about how your store is organized and be aware of the potential for impulse purchases as a result.

6

Trimming the Excess from Your Food Budget

W hile the focus of this book is on ways to cut back on what we already buy, we do have notable tips for making lifestyle and activity changes. These are changes we have made, partly to save money but also because they were good choices for our families. These tips present alternatives and some complements to using coupons and shopping sales.

There is a lot of money-saving potential in our kitchens. We've found the most savings from changes we've made in four areas: using alternative foods, cutting out the convenience products, cooking efficiently, and reducing waste. All of the changes we mention in this chapter are changes we have accommodated in our lives because we wanted to. Pick and choose which changes your family's lifestyle will support.

Using Alternative Foods

The easiest way to cut back your budget is by replacing some more expensive items with less expensive alternatives. For example, we have cut back our meat consumption considerably. Meat is one of the more expensive foods in our budget. We first experimented with this by serving smaller portions and adding more grains, like pasta and rice, and extra vegetables. We did this a couple of times a week to ease our families into it. The next step we took was to cut the meat from our meals completely a couple of nights a week. We added beans, eggs, and tofu to our diets (again, slowly). These foods are inexpensive, excellent sources of replacement protein, and highly versatile.

> $ **Centsable Tip** $
>
> This dietary change served two purposes: cutting our costs and providing a healthy alternative protein source. It also broadened our families' tastes and taught us to cook for our families in many new ways!

Cooking with seasonal fresh fruits and vegetables is a great way to save money on produce, and most of these items can be frozen for later use. When bananas and strawberries are in season, we use those in place of the more expensive blueberries to make muffins, waffles, and pancakes. If there are some left over that we won't use right away, we slice and freeze them for another day. We might puree many fruits or vegetables and package them in quarter-cup portions for freezing. We use these purees in desserts and main dish recipes from two creative chefs, Jessica Seinfeld, author of *Deceptively Delicious*, and Missy Chase Lapine, author of

The Sneaky Chef and *The Sneaky Chef to the Rescue*, to sneak a little more vegetables in our kids' diets. This trick even works on adults. Not long ago, Chrissy made her father his favorite potato soup recipe and included pureed cauliflower to add a little something extra. Chrissy's father typically refuses to eat cauliflower, but after the first bowl he declared it was the best potato soup he'd ever had! It's Chrissy's little secret!

> I started a meat-free night once a week because I wanted to help cut my grocery budget and improve my family's health. I tried to start with meals my family already loved and just skip the meat. I made meatless chili, tacos, and lasagna. Once my family was used to a meatless meal I moved on to try new recipes!
>
> —Becky

Cook for Your Health!

A big money-saving tip, and one we continue to focus on in our own homes, is avoiding prepackaged foods whenever possible. Prepackaged foods are more expensive per serving than homemade. When we purchase these products we pay for packaging, advertising, shipping, and the added preservatives to extend their shelf life. While we won't deny we love a great bargain, we have passed up many deals that didn't fit with our more important goal: a healthy family. Many prepackaged foods are high in added sugar, fat, and sodium. There are usually additives and preservatives and artificial coloring and flavoring. Having control over the ingredients of our meals is an important factor for us when we consider purchasing any foods. Prepackaged goods, while convenient, are not the mainstays of the healthy diet we are trying to achieve. So we decided to start making most of our foods from scratch (or as close to scratch as we can get with two little kids running around the kitchen!). The great thing is that our overall budget is lower because of it.

Having this control over ingredients also helps manage dietary restrictions with ease. For Kristin, maintaining a pantry stocked with prepackaged gluten-free foods would be a monumental and expensive task. Gluten-free foods are still primarily a specialty food. Buying them can sometimes cost more than twice what she'd pay for the alternative and they are not always high in nutritional value. Cooking items from scratch allows Kristin to save money and still provide healthy meals without the stuff that makes her children feel bad.

Cooking foods at home from fresh ingredients already in our kitchens nearly always tastes better! Remember Grandma's home cookin'? Mmm, mmm! We love it so much because grandmothers tended to cook from scratch with fresh foods. Our family members feel special when we spend time making a meal or snack just for them, just the way they like it. The great thing is, eliminating the prepackaged stuff doesn't mean we are actually spending more time cooking, and when we are it doesn't have to take all day. But, shhh . . . no one needs to know this! We have a few tips to help get cooks in and out of the kitchen as quickly as possible.

Get Started with Breakfast

The simplest and most important meal of the day is an easy place to start saving money. Breakfast cereal can get boring. Despite the fact that our children actually want cereal every day, we are moms and we know that eventually we will meet with rebellion (and we get tired of serving the same old cereal, too!). We found some easy ways to offer healthy variety for breakfast without breaking out the frying pan or serving up a three-course meal, and we still manage to save money.

For example, we add hot cereal to our menu once or twice a week. Hot cereals are inexpensive, they have enormous health benefits, they are filling, and they're extremely versatile. We use oatmeal by itself, in muffins and pancakes, and even in special meals liked Baked Oatmeal (see our website for links to great money-saving recipes like that one). We have found the easiest way to get hot cereal, specifically oatmeal, on the table in a hurry is to make a double or triple batch of it in the Crock-Pot overnight; we save what's left over for another meal. To spice it up even further, we add some chopped-up fruit, milk, and honey or cinnamon. Once a month or so we also make up an extra-large batch of pancake, waffle, or muffin batter and make two or three different kinds at once. We then freeze the leftovers for breakfasts throughout the month. This offers variety in a hurry and we spend less time in the kitchen. We'll talk more about this type of cooking later in the chapter. Egg puffs made with pureed sweet potatoes, yogurt and fruit parfaits, and smoothies are all filling, healthy, and easy to whip together. They can be made from ingredients we buy on sale and store in the freezer.

Unwrap Lunches and Snacks

Lunch is the meal that needs the most help around our homes and it's also the meal we are most likely to buy convenience foods for. Lunch falls in the middle of the day when we are busiest. We are either making lunch early in the morning when everyone is headed out the door or trying to get it ready with hungry toddlers on our hands. Packaged cookies, crackers, and even cheese are quick ways to fill a lunch box and empty a wallet. Speaking of costs, we were amazed recently to learn what the average family spends on "disposable lunches." The website www.wastefreelunches.org estimates it's around $724 a year! There are many great products to help make the switch to a waste-free lunch fun for the whole family. We started with a basic lunch cooler, reusable dishes, and water bottles. We have since moved on to environmentally friendly reusable sandwich and snack bags, stainless steel water bottles, BPA-free containers, washable napkins, and even unbreakable plates and utensils for picnic-type outings.

Sometimes it's just easier to eat out! We don't often think of it, but this is also a convenience food purchase, and we pay extra for the services of seating, preparation, cooking, serving, and cleanup. We combat these lunchtime traps through meal planning and preparation. Since deciding we needed to cut back on disposable and convenience foods, both for the sake of our budget and the environment, we have found many ways to make lunch convenient without paying extra to do it. The first big step to cutting these costs is to simply stop eating out. Now, really, we know we won't stop altogether but we can aim to lessen convenience meals born of underpreparation.

We've found it easiest to pack lunches at night because it makes mornings less stressful. This is especially helpful when we are planning to take leftovers. Packing up meals for lunch right after dinner actually helps clean up the kitchen, cuts down on the number of dishes needed to store the foods, and helps us remember to actually eat the leftovers before they are lost forever in the back of the refrigerator. Rather than throwing together whatever we can grab in the morning, we have time to put some thought into what we will eat the next day: plenty of snacks and a full lunch. It is healthier and less expensive.

Another easy way to cut the cost of convenience is to make and package snacks at home. There are great, very simple recipes for trail mix, granola bars, and crackers and cookies that save us a ton by cutting out the packaging and are still convenient when we are packing up and on the go. We make this a family activity, and our kids love to help us bake up a special treat. Yogurt, pudding, and Jell-O can all be made or purchased in larger quantities and dished up into single servings for lunches and snacks, and we see big savings. We even manage to get good fresh vegetables into our children by cutting them in advance into snack-size pieces and offering a healthy dip. They love these because they are fun and easy.

Dinner Savings

Most parents would agree, dinnertime is usually stressful. Dinner at Kristin's house is no different. Just when it's time to get the food started, her children seem to fall apart: fighting, crying, talking back . . . it's the "whining hour." To make this time of the day calmer, we both plan our menus and try to cook in advance. We may only get one or two meals prepared in advance but that's one or two afternoons that are calm and happy. We can read to the kids or play a game to keep them occupied before dinner. We have two different ways to eliminate dinnertime pressure: first, any chopping, dicing, or mixing that can be done in advance we do on the weekend or in the morning, when time is more flexible and tempers are more agreeable; and second, we try to cook once for two or three meals at at time, simultaneously, whenever possible. We talked a little bit about this in the menu-planning section in chapter 4 and it's such a big help that it's worth mentioning again. Chrissy often cooks up a double batch of ground turkey in several different ways and freezes it for later. For example, in the same night she could cook up all the meat necessary to make spaghetti, chili, meatballs, and meat loaf! It takes a little bit longer to do this but she already has the oven and stove on and the kitchen messy and it will save her double the time on a busy night down the road. In addition, she can often save money by buying a much larger package of meat at one time versus two or three smaller packages. We recommend practicing these cooking methods with meals your family already knows and likes, and that are easy to prepare. Below, we offer specific tips on cooking in bulk.

Don't Repeat Our Mistake

Kristin once spent an entire evening making up three pans of a new lasagna recipe to freeze and eat while her family was packing for a cross-country move. Her family didn't care for the new version of the lasagna and she was left with two full unwanted pans in the freezer taking up valuable space. What a waste!

Cooking at home takes time and preparation and we know (really, we do!) that there's not always a lot of time available. The best way to combat a daily busy schedule (when it comes to cooking, anyway) is to do as much ahead of time as possible. For example, make a point of washing or preparing produce as soon as it comes home from the store. Chop anything that will be used for snacks, wash and dry fruits and veggies your family will want to grab and eat on the go, and store everything in the proper containers.

Crock-Pots are another great time and money saver. We try to remember to use our Crock-Pot in the summertime to save energy by keeping the house cooler. We have discovered that just about anything can be cooked in a Crock-Pot.

Have a Bulk Cooking Day!

We cook in bulk several different ways. Sometimes it's simply a "cook once, eat twice" approach; other times we cook a full week's worth of food; and once in a while we feel really ambitious and cook a full month's worth of meals in one weekend.

Here are some tips to make this activity as painless as possible.

We usually cook in bulk on the weekends, when our husbands are home to take care of the kids, and we always have a meal plan. Bulk cooking requires a little more preparation than a regular meal plan. Some ingredients for a meal cannot be cooked ahead, for example, and others need to be combined at certain points in the process. We plan our meals and write down the actual cooking steps. This is an extra step, but it saves time and helps us organize our cooking in the most logical order.

Plan the Cooking Process

1. Which items must be prepared or cooked first?
2. Which recipes have the same ingredients? We can prepare it once for all the recipes.
3. Which items will take the longest and shortest time to cook? This helps stagger cooking and preparation to make the most efficient use of our time.
4. Are there any meals that can be baked in the oven at the same time?

Prepare the Kitchen

We gather all of our ingredients at once and arrange the kitchen in stations (one area for chopping, one for mixing, a large bowl or trash can for waste, and a sink full of water for washing and collecting dirty dishes). Speaking of dirty dishes, we clean as we go. The last thing anyone wants to do after an entire afternoon of cooking is to clean!

Allow Foods to Cool Before Placing Them in Storage Containers

We recommend storing items in the freezer in flat freezer bags, or in glass containers with an airtight lid, labeled with the name of the meal, any instructions for cooking, and preparation date.

Write It Down!

The last thing we do is write down what's in the freezer, along with a use-by date (approximate freezer life of each meal). We both use a dry erase board in our kitchen for this list. It's in an easy-to-see spot, so anytime we are trying to figure out "what's for dinner," we can check the list. We like to include leftovers and snacks on there, too!

Bulk cooking is a great way to save money even after cutting back with coupons and sales.

> I had been using coupons and store incentives to cut my family's grocery bill. I thought I couldn't cut my budget any more but then I read about bulk cooking and how much time and money I could save and tried it! I am able to stock up on loss leaders, then plan and cook meals around them. We save time and money and my family thinks I am Superwoman because they have a home-cooked meal every night!
>
> —*Monica*

The most difficult thing about bulk cooking is creating enough variety without creating a lot of extra work. One easy way to do this is to cook a large batch of a basic recipe, then divide it up and add a twist. We often do this with pancakes, sauces, and ground meats. One month Chrissy made triple the pancake batter, divided it into thirds, then flavored each third differently and cooked and froze them. Her family was amazed she had time to make a new variety of pancakes every week! Kristin's kids love chicken fingers so after finding a great gluten-free recipe that was baked rather than fried, she wanted to cut out some of the extra work while still giving her kids the food they love. She makes up four to six pounds of chicken fingers at once, uses some the same evening for dinner, and freezes the rest for two additional meals down the road. They might have orange chicken with veggies and rice, breaded chicken salad with dressing, or barbecue chicken wraps the next time. All it takes is a little thawing and reheating.

Now that our food is cooked and we've cut out time spent in the kitchen, we want to make sure it's all used to feed our family and not fill the landfill. According to a study by the University of Arizona, a family of four wastes as much as $500 a year in foods they throw away. Much of this can be saved with proper storage and use of leftovers.

Proper Food Storage

There are many ways to be sure food in the refrigerator and freezer stay fresh and healthy for as long as possible. First, be sure the refrigerator temperature is correct; it should be between 35 and 38 degrees Fahrenheit. Freezers should be set at 0 degrees Fahrenheit or lower. Allow foods to cool before storing them in the refrigerator (but be sure to get them there within two hours). Warm or hot foods will create condensation, which can decrease the quality of the food, contribute to mold growth, and make the refrigerator or freezer work harder. Warm foods also let off more odors than cold foods. Airtight lids and wrapping keep foods fresh longer. Air and odors can degrade the quality of leftovers and other foods in the refrigerator and freezer.

Storing foods in the best location in refrigerators and freezers is important as well. Crisper drawers and meat drawers claim to control humidity but we simply look at this as a suggestion. The best tips we have found are to store foods in the refrigerator by their cooking temperature: ready-to-eat foods and leftovers on the top shelf; raw meats near or at the bottom (where it's typically colder); dairy, eggs, and cheese at the back near the top; dressings and condiments on the door. We try to keep fruits and vegetables separated because fruit gives off a gas that causes many vegetables to spoil more quickly. Finally, there are several fruits and vegetables that don't need to be refrigerated at all.

ACCORDING TO THE UNIVERSITY OF CALIFORNIA–DAVIS (HTTP://HOMEORCHARD.UCDAVIS.EDU/FVSTORAGE. PDF), THE FOLLOWING PRODUCE SHOULD BE LEFT AT ROOM TEMPERATURE, ON A PANTRY SHELF OR IN A FRUIT BASKET, AND EATEN WHEN RIPE:

Apples (for seven days or less)
Bananas
Cantaloupe
Cucumbers
Eggplant
Fresh basil (with stems in water)
Garlic
Ginger
Grapefruit

Jicama

Lemons

Limes

Mandarins

Mangoes

Onions (but not scallions)

Oranges

Papayas

Peppers

Persimmons

Pineapples

Plantains

Pomegranates

Potatoes

Pumpkins

Sweet potatoes

Tomatoes

Watermelons

Winter squash

For best results, store garlic, onions, potatoes, and sweet potatoes in a well-ventilated area in the pantry. Protect potatoes from light to avoid greening. Cucumbers, eggplant, and peppers can be kept in the refrigerator for one to three days if they are used soon after removal from the refrigerator.

Reduce Food Waste

Once we've taken such efforts to save time and money, we want to be sure it doesn't go to waste. Some families (or family members) aren't thrilled with the idea of leftovers. To combat this, we often incorporate our leftovers into a new recipe. It's simple to find recipes online and, unless we tell our kids, they don't know! A night or two before vacation or a trip to the grocery store, we have a "clean out the fridge" meal to free up space and reduce waste.

Action Plan

1. Pick two expensive items that you cook with, and come up with less expensive alternatives you can use as substitutes for them.
2. Think of one prepackaged item your family currently uses, and start preparing and/or packaging it yourself at home.
3. Check out BeCentsable.net for:
   a. Links to a wide variety of waste-free lunch options.
   b. Help with food storage and bulk cooking.
   c. More food storage information.

7

Cleaning Up Your Budget

Now that we have laid out a plan for how to save on groceries, it's time to start looking at other ways to save around the house that may seem small, but can have a big impact.

Cleaning our homes is not something we love to do; we like a clean house, just not the work it takes to get it clean. All of the cleaning products for sale on store shelves are developed and marketed to make the chore of housekeeping seem easier and more enjoyable. What most people don't consider is the price we pay for this at the register.

Cleaning products have been commercialized to make us think they are a necessity. If we don't have toilet cleaner, how on earth do we keep the toilet clean? What do we use on the floors? The windows and mirrors? And we absolutely cannot do laundry without the fresh-smelling detergent formulated just for our washing machines. That's not to say we don't need something to clean our bathrooms, floors, windows, and clothes, but most of us just don't need what we think we do. We certainly don't need the prices attached to those items. Trust us, we are former "if it doesn't smell like a woodland forest it's not clean" groupies!

Most of our great cleaning discoveries were inspired by the birth of our first-born children. We wanted products that would be safe for our kids as they began exploring their world. As our children grew older we hated the battle that ensued when it was time to clean anything. A toddler *must* do whatever Mom or Dad does, and we hated the idea of cleaning with all those chemicals in the same room as our kids.

We were honestly shocked to learn that most of the products on the market had inadequate labels. Because of trade secret laws, the FDA does not require ingredients labels to include every ingredient in the actual product.[1] This is a great way to protect manufacturers but makes it very hard for consumers to know what they are buying. We also discovered that "most chemicals used in consumer products have never undergone federal safety review. In fact, the Environmental Protection Agency (EPA) has required testing for fewer than 200 of the 62,000 chemicals used in commerce since the agency began reviewing chemicals in 1979."[2] So even if there was adequate labeling in place, we still wouldn't know if the ingredients were safe because most of them have not been properly tested. This is the reason we put our money-saving skills to work, looking for creative ways to apply them to cleaning while achieving the safety we were looking for.

---

1   *Consumer Reports* GreenerChoices.org (www.greenerchoices.org/products
    .cfm?product=greencleaning&page=RightChoices).
2   *Consumer Reports* GreenerChoices.org (www.greenerchoices.org/products
    .cfm?product=greencleaning&page=WhyItMatters).

What Can You Do?

We began reading about and researching how to save money on eco-friendly, all-natural household cleaners. We found a solution we were very skeptical of at first: homemade cleaners. Our list of reasons against these products was long and seemed valid. We were busy moms with young children; making up batches of cleaning supplies would be just one more thing on our to-do lists. No, thank you!

We didn't believe any of the assertions made by people who swore by homemade cleaning agents. Were they really that easy and less expensive? Did they even work? We have messy children, messy dogs. After spaghetti night there's sauce on the tables, floors, walls, high chairs . . . we needed something really strong! And what did the cleaners smell like? If it isn't "mountain fresh," it isn't clean. Right?

Wrong again!

Ultimately, we decided to have an open mind. We felt it was important and it couldn't hurt to try. Luckily, in our quest for a healthy home, we also found a new way to cut our budget. We can provide a safe environment for our families, gain peace of mind for ourselves, keep the planet healthier, and save money . . . who wouldn't call that a winning combination?

Do We Have the Time and Skills?

We were first surprised at how easy the cleaners were to make and how little time it took. It only takes about one minute to make an all-purpose cleaner that saves more than $2.50 a bottle compared to all-purpose cleaners like Lysol or Fantastik!

Does It Really Cost Less?

The primary ingredient in most cleaning products is water.[3] So when we buy a bottle of all-purpose cleaner we are really paying for a little bit of cleaning chemical (that's not regulated and possibly toxic), a lot of water, and some pretty packaging, plus advertising and shipping. The products we make are still mostly water, but we aren't paying for the pretty packaging and we know exactly what's in the bottle!

Does It Work?

Our next cleaning challenge was performance. Do homemade cleaners really work as well as commercial cleaners? Believe it or not, they work better! We've mentioned our four-legged family members, the dogs. Between us we have four of them, and as anyone with dogs knows, dog slobber on windows is like superglue! With a popular commercial glass cleaner it took quite a bit of scrubbing, but with our homemade mixture it was amazingly easy. The natural acidity of vinegar (the main ingredient in our homemade cleaners) breaks down foods and other sticky, gooey, gluey substances, and dog slobber!

What about Disinfecting? Do Homemade Cleaners Kill Bacteria?

A valid concern we hear from many people (most often concerned mothers) is regarding germs and bacteria. Antibacterial products are quite common on store shelves. But numerous studies conducted over the past few years have suggested that these products

3   Swiffer (www.swiffer.com/en_US/pet_health.do).

may actually be increasing the development of "superbugs" (those resistant to common antibiotics).

Many of the products we will tell you about can be used separately or in conjunction with one another as an effective disinfectant. Specifically hydrogen peroxide, vinegar, and the properly combined use of the two (we describe the method later in this chapter). The Virginia Polytechnic Institute and State University found that this kills almost all salmonella, shigella, and E. coli bacteria and is more effective than chlorine bleach or any commercially available cleaner.[4]

Where's My "Mountain Fresh" Scent?

We have been programmed to believe that "clean" is a scent. Actually, some products even tout "clean" as their scent. Remember, clean is a state, not a smell! Fragrances added to commercial cleaners are just more chemicals we bring into our homes. The presence of many chemicals can be masked on product labels by simply categorizing them as "fragrance."[5]

Serendipitous Results

When we use homemade cleaners, we are not only protecting our families and our own health, we are protecting the environment. We are reducing the toxins released into the air, water, and soil

4   Examiner.com   (www.examiner.com/x-12736-Tampa-Health-and-Beauty
    -Examiner~y2009m6d26-Prevent-ecoli-illnesses-from-crosscontaminations
    -in-your-kitchen).
5   EWG's   Enviroblog   (www.enviroblog.org//2007/12/ask-ewg-what-is
    -fragrance.html).

during production, use, and disposal of the commercial products. We keep our homemade cleaners in reusable containers, and the individual ingredients we purchase to make the cleaners go a long way for only a little money.

Before we share our favorite homemade cleaner recipes, we'll introduce the key ingredients and some general guidelines.

How to Get Started

It's important to always label homemade cleaners. Even though they are natural and mostly safe, some can still cause skin, respiratory, and intestinal irritation, especially for children and pets.

Homemade cleaners are made from items most everyone will find in their pantry. They are inexpensive and easy to mix up in just a couple of minutes. Here is a list of household pantry items and their uses:

Vinegar: A disinfectant and all-purpose cleaner, it cuts grease and will kill a fair amount of mold and mildew.

Baking soda: A naturally abrasive powder, it can kill bacteria and mildew, and it does not scratch glass.

Borax: A naturally occurring mineral composed of sodium, boron, oxygen, and water, it can be used safely in washing machines and to clean toilets.

Washing soda: A great all-purpose cleaner and laundry additive, it has uses similar to baking soda but can scratch some surfaces.

Castile soap: A soap made from vegetable oil rather than animal fat or synthetic substances, it can be used as total body cleaner, laundry soap, and dish soap.

Lemon juice: Naturally acidic, it has antiseptic and antibacterial properties, freshens and cleans well, and removes stains.

Note of Caution: Although borax and washing soda are derived from naturally occurring substances, they can still cause eye and respiratory irritation. Take caution when handling these or any un-ingestible substance.

The items above are easy to find and inexpensive. Even castile soap, which most families have not seen or used before, is very easy to find. We use these products, combined in various ways, to clean our homes on a daily basis. They are effective, inexpensive, and healthier for our families.

> Before I discovered homemade cleaners, I spent so much money on commercial products to get my house clean. I was so surprised when I tried homemade cleaners and found they clean just as well without the harmful chemicals. I can't believe how much money I have wasted over the years on expensive cleaners when I could have been making my own!
>
> —*Emily*

In addition to all the liquids, powders, scrubs, and solvents used to clean our homes, we also have a lot of "tools" we whip out when there's a mess to clean up. Paper towels, disposable dusting cloths, disposable floor mops, and disposable toilet bowl cleaning pads. These items not only add to our budget but also to landfills and pollution levels. We realized after months of shopping centsably that purchases of these products in particular were among the most difficult to save money on. Even a good deal was still a lot of money out of our pockets that we didn't have to spend. But, we wondered, how could we manage all of life's messes without them?

Our first really big change was to stop using paper towels for kitchen cleanup. Cloth towels are inexpensive and actually do a much better job for less than a quarter of the cost. Cloth towels cost us about $25 a year. The average family spends $180 a year just on paper towels! Using cloth towels does require a tad bit more water and detergent usage but the amount is minimal compared to the savings. To make this change in our kitchens we found a spot under the sink or in a drawer for a small basket or other container. We placed the towels in the room where we'd need them, where they would be easy to reach and easy to use; this makes the transition less painful. These towels are kind of earmarked for the kitchen so when we do laundry we know where they go. We try to choose darker colors to minimize staining and lengthen their useful life. Chrissy also uses two different colors, one for each of her children, to stop the spread of germs. Be sure to hang wet towels to dry to avoid mildew and odors.

This change was so easy to make and such a money saver, we started thinking about what other disposable products we could eliminate. Pretreated dusting and mopping cloths and window cleaning wipes were next on the list. Kristin's husband had a serious (and unwavering) affinity for those fluffy little disposable dusters. He was the ultimate critic. We purchased several microfiber cloths and mitts and were amazed at how easy the transition was. The microfiber cloths don't leave lint behind and they trap the dust and dirt easily so we aren't redepositing it around the house. These cloths and mitts cost around $8 (for a mitt or a pack of three or four cloths) and they last all year. The packs of pretreated wipes and dusters cost $3–$5 each and we were buying them every month. Microfiber mop heads are a phenomenal improvement over pretreated pads or traditional mop heads, and, like the cloths and mitts, they can be tossed in the washer to clean. The microfiber materials clean our furniture, floors, and mirrors much better than any of the other products we had been using.

In the next section we will detail the best-performing homemade cleaners room by room and then recommend some commercially available "green" cleaners.

The Kitchen

The kitchens in our homes require a strong **all-purpose cleaner** (to get all those sticky fingerprints off!). We simply mix a solution of equal parts distilled white vinegar and water in a clean spray bottle. The vinegar does have an odor but it dissipates after just a few minutes and leaves no residue or lingering scent. Essential oils can be added to mask the vinegar odor. This solution costs us about 30¢ a bottle to make (not including the bottle purchase). You can get a spray bottle for around a dollar or just reuse one you already have (be sure to clean repurposed bottles and sprayers well and label them clearly).

ALL-PURPOSE CLEANER

1 part vinegar
1 part water
Essential oil (optional)

Dishwasher detergent is another expense we have found a way around. Combine equal parts borax and washing soda, mix well, and store in an airtight container. Use just one tablespoonful per load. This leaves our dishes spot free and is easier on our dishwashers.

DISHWASHING DETERGENT

1 part borax
1 part washing soda
Use just one tablespoonful per load.

$ **Centsable Tip** $

More is not better with the dishwashing detergent.
Be sure to use just one tablespoon!

To **clean our microwaves** we used to use multipurpose cleaners
and still had to scrub and scrub to get the small baked-on bits off.
Imagine our joy when we discovered a cleaner that didn't require
any scrubbing. Here's the secret: lemons! Just place half a lemon in
a small bowl of water, and microwave for thirty to sixty seconds
(just enough time to bring the water to a light boil and build up
steam). Open the door and wipe with a wet towel or sponge. Easy
as pie—and you could clean that off, too!

The Bathroom

We talked earlier about **glass cleaner** and how much we loved the
homemade version we tried. This homemade glass cleaner is the
same recipe as the all-purpose cleaner we use in the kitchen.

GLASS CLEANER

1 part vinegar
1 part water
Essential oil (optional)

The really gross stuff in our homes requires the most dangerous
chemicals to clean. Or so we thought. The **toilets and drains**—
yuck! These cleaners are among the most hazardous in any home.
When Chrissy looked up her toilet cleaner on the U.S. Department
of Health and Human Services' Household Products Database

(http://householdproducts.nlm.nih.gov/index.htm), what she found shocked her. They recommended she wear long rubber gloves and eye protection! The product was corrosive to the eyes and skin and required emergency medical attention if it came in contact with any body part. We felt as though we needed full body armor just to clean our bathrooms. This made the run-of-the-mill bathroom germs seem pretty benign!

A safer, less expensive way to clean drains and toilets is a simple solution of vinegar and baking soda. We sprinkle one-half cup baking soda in our drain or toilet bowl, add one-half cup of vinegar, and let it sit for a half hour (or overnight, in the toilet). In drains, we then pour a full cup of hot water down to rinse; in the toilet bowl, we scrub with the toilet brush and flush.

TOILET CLEANER

½ cup baking soda
½ cup vinegar
Let sit (for at least a half hour). Scrub, then flush.

DRAIN CLEANER

½ cup baking soda
½ cup vinegar
1 cup hot water
Pour the baking soda in the drain, add the vinegar, and let it sit for a half hour. Then pour the hot water down to rinse.

We **clean our tubs** with baking soda or washing soda as well (just be careful when using washing soda on fiberglass tub inserts, as it can scratch them). Mix the powder with water to form a paste and scrub. Be sure to rinse well; the soda leaves a residue if it's not rinsed completely. The first time Kristin tried this she couldn't believe how easy and cheap it was to clean her tub. She always used to worry about giving her kids a bath after using chemicals to clean her tub, but not anymore!

TUB CLEANER

3 parts baking soda or washing soda
1 part water
Scrub and rinse.

Speaking of germs, a great whole-house **disinfectant** is a two-step spraying of hydrogen peroxide and vinegar. These products are virtually harmless to human beings and pets and more effective than bleach at killing germs and bacteria.[6] The chemical reaction that occurs when the two products are combined on surfaces creates pure oxygen. No immunity can be built up against pure oxygen.

Simply fill one spray bottle with vinegar and one opaque spray bottle with hydrogen peroxide (be sure this is an opaque bottle). Spray one, then the other, on any hard surface and wipe clean. Be sure not to mix these substances in the same bottle or they will become ineffective (note that this is not effective against viruses like the flu).

DISINFECTANT CLEANER

Fill one spray bottle with vinegar.
Fill one opaque spray bottle with hydrogen peroxide.
Spray one, then the other, on any hard surface and wipe clean.

---

6   *Natural Home* (www.naturalhomemagazine.com/article.aspx?id=1742&
    ekfxmen_noscript=1&ekfxmensel=e0fa05764_48_66&page=3).

> **$ Centsable Tip $**
>
> It can be difficult to find empty opaque spray bottles, so we buy the largest bottle of hydrogen peroxide available and reuse a trigger spray from an old cleaner (we make sure to clean it well first by spraying a full bottle of plain, hot water through it).

Finding Money in the Laundry (That's Always Fun!)

The laundry room is where we hit the jackpot! **Laundry detergent** is so expensive. The brand-name detergents cost around 27¢ a load. We used to use one of the less expensive brands but we found they are not as effective and only save us about 5¢–10¢ a load.[7] Now, imagine doing a load of laundry for 1¢ or 2¢ a load. It's possible and so simple and it amounts to big savings, considering we do at least ten loads a week. We're saving over $100 a year on laundry, creating a healthier home and helping the environment at the same time.

We were reluctant to try this, thinking it would take too much time and probably not get our clothes clean. But after seeing a short video online of the process . . . well, you probably know where this is going. We were wrong again! The detergent works as well as the name brands we were buying, costs us 90% less, and only takes ten minutes of our time every other month to make. That's actually less time than it would take to go to the store to buy a new bottle of detergent.

7   *Consumer Reports*, July 2009 (www.consumerreports.org/cro/magazine-archive/july-2009/home-garden/laundry-detergents/ratings/laundry-detergents-ratings.htm).

Thanks to BeCentsable I learned how to make my own laundry detergent that only costs 1¢ a load. I was skeptical that this recipe would take too long to make or be too complicated. I was surprised at how easy the recipe was. This laundry soaps works even better than the brand-name soap I used to buy!

—*Angela*

LAUNDRY DETERGENT[8]

About 3 ounces of bar soap, grated. Any bar of soap will do but we like to stick with all-natural bar soaps, like Castile; don't be concerned with the scent, as it washes away in the laundry.
½ cup borax
½ cup washing soda
Prepare as directed below. Use one-half cup per load.

In a large pot combine 6 cups of water with grated soap and heat on medium until the soap is melted. Stir in borax and washing soda until everything is dissolved. In a large bucket place 4 cups of hot water and then add your soap mix. Stir well and then add 1 gallon plus 6 cups of water. Stir again and then let sit overnight. The detergent will be a watery gel that might look cloudy.

We also found some ways to save money and still get our clothes soft and static free. One easy way to double the life of a box of dryer sheets is to cut them in half. We also skip dryer sheets altogether during the summer months (some climates are much more arid

8 Adapted from Crystal Miller, "Making Homemade Laundry Soap" (www.thefamilyhomestead.com/laundrysoap.htm).

so this is not desirable) or we add 1 cup of distilled white vinegar to our washload (don't worry, the vinegar smell goes away in the wash!).

Vinegar is also great laundry booster. We add 1 cup vinegar to the rinse water. This product is a true multitasker: it whitens, brightens, softens, and neutralizes odors![9]

Removing stains is always tough, but again, we already have in our cupboards safe alternatives that work just as well as the commercial products.

Salt: grease and blood remover—just sprinkle on and let sit for a few minutes, brush salt off, and wash (repeat if necessary until stain is gone)

Rubbing alcohol: grass stain remover

Liquid dish detergent: all-purpose stain remover (especially food stains)

Liquid laundry detergent: a great pretreater—just fill a spray bottle with liquid laundry soap to treat stains on the spot

Pretreater: a mix of ½ cup hydrogen peroxide, ½ cup baking soda, and 1 cup hot water; let stand overnight

---

$ **Centsable Tip** $

With all stains, our success rate is greater when we catch the stain as soon as possible after it happens. These treatments work best in those instances. If we are away from home, we try to keep the stain wet until we can get home to treat it.

---

9   Frugal Living, About.com: Frugal Living (http://frugalliving.about.com/od/colthing/qt/Laundry_Booster.htm).

The Proof Is in the Living Room

Last but not least, we have even found ways to save on **furniture polish and floor care**. Commercially produced furniture polishes contain chemicals for scent and consistency and alcohol to help them dry. What our wood furniture really needs is an oil-based treatment to keep the wood from drying and cracking. For general dusting of artificial or manufactured wood we use either a vacuum cleaner with the brush attachment or a lightly dampened microfiber or microfleece towel. For polishing our wood furniture we like to use a mixture containing pure olive oil to prolong its life. We simply mix our ingredients in a spritzer bottle, spray some on our towel, and polish away! Easy and very inexpensive.

FURNITURE POLISH

2 tablespoons lemon juice
1 drop olive oil
1 pint (16 ounces) vinegar

$　　　**Centsable Tip**　　$

Be sure to shake the furniture polish mixture well before each use. Even the small amount of oil will separate from the vinegar and lemon juice.

Properly caring for your hard floors is so easy it will likely surprise you. Most materials, natural or synthetic, will last longer and look better cleaned with a simple solution of mild dish soap and hot water. We recommend a good mop with a flat head and several (two or three) microfiber pads. These are not expensive but it's

important to find a strong handle that's not too heavy and a head
that swivels easily and isn't overly large.

FLOOR CLEANER

¼ cup mild dish soap
1 gallon warm water

Cleaning carpets is an arduous, unfriendly task. To keep carpets clean for as long as possible, we each implemented a "no shoes"
policy. Shoes come off at the door, we all have special backyard play
shoes that stay outdoors, and even our little toddlers understand to
remove those shoes before they come in the house. It's easier than
you may think and helps keep the house clean in a number of ways.
First, it eliminates tracked-in mud or other gunky outdoor things
we won't think about. Second, our carpets stay cleaner. Third, our
shoes are always together, by the door when we are ready to leave.
This is especially helpful for the little ones, who always seem to be
missing a shoe somewhere! To start this routine, simply round up
or purchase some small baskets, bins, or buckets, or even a small
shoe shelf, and place one by each exterior door of your home.
Everyone slips their shoes off when they arrive home; they may
even want to keep a pair of slippers handy by the doors to wear
around the house, especially in the colder months.

In the event that a carpet stain makes its way into our homes
(it's a shocker, really!) we are armed with easy ways to take care
of it. The best treatment we have used is that vinegar and water
solution, the all-purpose cleaner from earlier in this chapter. We
soak up as much of the stain-causing liquid as we can, spray the
cleaning solution on the spot liberally, let it sit for ten to twenty
minutes, then soak it up with a damp towel (tougher stains may
require more elbow grease). This has worked on every stain we've

had to treat. Since we have dogs at home we also have odors to deal with, specifically when it's rainy or humid. An easy fix for that is to sprinkle baking soda directly on the carpet (make sure the carpet is dry or it will clump and turn to cement!) and let sit for at least thirty minutes, and then just vacuum it up.

CARPET CLEANER

1 part vinegar
1 part water
Combine in a spray or squirt bottle and shake well.

Commercial Cleaners

We mainly use homemade cleaners in our homes but we realize that's not something everyone wants to do. Most "green" commercial cleaners are more expensive than the homemade versions but we have found some commercial cleaners that are a good buy. We were even able to find a better and less expensive glass cleaner than the homemade version (if that's even possible). Shaklee's Basic H^2 is highly concentrated and the cleaner made from it only costs 1¢ a bottle (no, that's not a typo, just one penny!). We were skeptical at first because it only requires a very small amount of cleaner mixed with a full spray bottle of water, but we tried it and we're sold.

Here is a list of our favorite commercially available green cleaners.

ARM AND HAMMER ESSENTIALS

- Type of cleaner: laundry detergent
- Available at: most retail stores

- Retail cost: $2.50–$5.00
- Product is made from biodegradable plant-based soaps, is free of dyes, contains no phosphates or bleaches, and is boosted by baking soda.

CAPTURE CARPET CLEANER

- Type of cleaner: carpet
- Available at: most home improvement stores
- Retail cost: $7–$20
- Product contains no bleach, solvents, or harsh chemicals.

DR. BRONNER'S

- Type of cleaner: general cleaning
- Available at: health food stores, some general retail stores including Target, and online
- Retail cost: $4–$10
- Many products are concentrated. One bottle can be used to make many bottles of cleaner.
- Certified organic by the USDA National Organic Program; certified as "fair trade" under the IMO's Fair for Life program; cruelty free.

SEVENTH GENERATION

- Type of cleaners: dish and laundry
- Available at: health food stores and some general retail stores
- Retail cost: $4–$10
- Products are nontoxic; have no dyes, fragrances, or chlorine; contain no petroleum-based cleaners or phosphates; are safe

for septic and gray-water systems; are certified kosher; and are not tested on animals.

SHAKLEE

- Type: general cleaning
- Available: online
- Retail cost: $8–$12
- Many products are concentrated. One bottle can be used to make many bottles of cleaner. No harmful chemicals like parabens, ammonia, formaldehyde, or phthalates. Shaklee was the first company in the world to earn Climate Neutral certification for totally offsetting its greenhouse gas emissions, resulting in a net zero impact on the environment.

It's important to point out that we made these changes in our homes over the course of a full year. Don't feel overwhelmed or consumed by the idea that you need to do all of this at once. Follow the game plan below and you'll see results!

Action Plan

1. Examine the cleaning products around your home.
   a. Think about what product you'd most like to stop buying:
      i. Is it expensive?
      ii. Is it a safety concern?
   b. Choose one to change this week, just one.
2. Now try a homemade recipe to replace that one product, and compare its performance to the product you were using.

a. You may also want to try comparing the homemade products against store-bought "green" cleaners (check our website for options).

b. Which one did you like better?

3. Now go back to step one and pick another product to change. Before you know it, you'll be green and centsable!

4. Check out BeCentsable.net to find out where to get all these great cleaners and supplies.

8

Utilities

Utilities are a large part of our monthly expenses and there is a lot we can do to save money on them. So much so that we feel it is necessary to devote an entire chapter to it.

The simple changes we will go over in this chapter can result in big savings.

We used to believe that if we wanted to enjoy the comforts of home, our utilities were a fixed expense that we really didn't have control over. We have to have air conditioning (we have to suffer through Arizona and Missouri in the middle of July), natural gas (who wants a cold shower every morning?), and running water (you won't find us pumping a well at dawn for a bath!). There really were no other options, unless we invested in solar panels and a windmill.

So, if we have to have these utilities, let's be smarter about how we use them!

With a new project on our hands, we delved into an area we had never considered when it came to controlling our expenses. Even if we had considered it, the changes we thought we'd have to make weren't really appealing.

It never occurred to us that by simply unplugging a few things and adjusting our thermostats a few degrees we could save significant money every month. Don't believe it? Keep reading!

Both of our families made many of the changes that we're going to discuss in this chapter. Chrissy's family was enrolled in a level-pay program with their electric and gas company (this is when the utility company averages your use over twelve months so you can pay a flat fee all year), paying $221 a month. After a full year with these changes in effect, their level-pay amount dropped to just $116 a month! That's nearly 50% savings, over $1,200 a year just on their utility bill!

Again, it's all about having the right knowledge and tools at hand and, of course, changing your thinking!

Understanding Utility Bills

In order to take control of something, we must understand how it works. When we decided to attack and conquer our utility bills, we took some time to call each of the companies and ask them to explain our bill to us. It was also important to find which appliances and systems in our home were using each type of energy. For example, is our clothes dryer gas or electric? Do we have an electric heat pump or an electric or gas-forced air furnace (or maybe a combination)? Are our homes equipped with a traditional gas water heater or a newer electric "tankless" system? The ins and outs of these systems, and their benefits, is an interesting topic but not one we will go into. What's important to know and understand is what your home is equipped with and how to manage the appropriate energy sources efficiently.

What Questions Did We Ask?
What Did We Find Out?

What are the units of measure?
We found this on our billing statements. The units are pretty standard across the country:

- Electric: Kilowatt-hours (kWh)
- Water: gallon, liter or cubic feet (ccf)
- Natural Gas: cubic feet (ccf), or therms (also referred to as BTU's)
- Propane: Pounds (lbs.)

What is the rate charged per unit?
Again, this was easily found on our statements. There is no way to measure a high rate versus a low rate. Since most energy companies have no competition, the rates are set by a board and the state has to approve them. Despite this, knowing our rate was still helpful for three reasons.

1. When we received those wonderful notices in the mail about utility rate increases, we were better able to understand the impact down to the penny that the increase would have on us.
2. After we did some investigating and understood our family's usage patterns, we were able to estimate potential savings.

3. We were knowledgeable about our electric company's seasonal and tiered usage rates and able to manage our activity around them.

Does the rate change during different times of the day, different seasons, or once a certain usage level is reached?

To get the answer to this question, we found it easiest to call our utility companies directly. Some companies have this information readily available on their websites; others do not. We learned some very interesting things.

Chrissy's electric company in Missouri charges a higher rate during different seasons and on the first 500 kWh used each month. From May to September Chrissy pays a peak-season rate. If she used 1,200 kWh in peak season and the same 1,200 kWh in non-peak season it would cost her $25 more a month in peak season just because the rates are higher.

In Arizona, Kristin's electric company offers several different programs. She has the option of prepaying for her service, paying one flat rate all the time, or rates based on the time of day the utility is being used, also called "time of use." The time-of-use programs usually require a special meter installation. All three programs are also subject to seasonal rate changes.

Other electric companies offer special voluntary programs, like "cycling," where the customer allows the utility company to power down his or her system remotely during emergencies or unusually high demand in exchange for a slightly reduced rate.

What did we do with this knowledge?

It's not so much what we did as how we did it. We still had an information gap to fill. Where could we make changes that would have the most impact? Were we directly using unnecessary energy or were we letting it escape? The only way to find out was to do an energy audit. We opted to do it ourselves but many electric companies will do them for a small fee or, if you are lucky, for free.

We used the federal government's Energy Star program (a collaborative effort between the Department of Energy and the Environmental Protection Agency), which offers a simple home energy audit. This tool also allowed us to compare our homes to homes in other states across the country and provided recommendations based on the results. The audit required a twelve-month utility bill history and the square footage of our home.

> $　　**Centsable Tip**　　$
>
> Don't put off the energy audit because your statements are not handy. Contact your utility companies; many of them will send a summary via mail or e-mail or even tell you usage and charges over the phone. You can also check their websites for account management options that usually include bill history.

The Game Plan: Spend $150 and Save $5,150 in Five Years!

Watch while we begin by spending just $150 and end up saving more than thirty-three times that! We'd never be able to make that much investing in the stock market! Our game plan spans five years because at that point several of the investments and improvements made around our homes will be ready for replacement. For all of the savings listed in this section, we've used data on average family usage to estimate savings. If there was no data available, we used our own family's savings as an estimate.

> I'm so thrilled this year to see that we've cut our energy usage in half! I had no idea that small, simple changes could save us so much. I'm so excited about the money we are saving, I've told everyone I know!
>
> —*Rose*

Investment #1

Switch twenty bulbs to CFL (compact fluorescent lamps) = *$70*
Five-year return: $1,700 ($340 a year)

Compact fluorescent lamps (CFLs) consume 75% less energy than traditional incandescent bulbs and last ten times longer (according to Energy Star). Lighting accounts for 20% of the average family's energy cost. Switching to CFLs will not only lower energy costs, it will conserve energy and cut down on greenhouse gas emissions.

Kristin's family began switching to CFLs in 2005 just before the birth of their first child. At the time, they were preparing a nursery in the spare bedroom. Because CFLs don't use as much energy, they also do not get hot to the touch, and the bulbs themselves are made of thicker glass. Kristin and her husband opted for a CFL for their nursery lamp. The lamp with the same CFL bulb they placed in it in 2005 has been through two toddlers, numerous drops and bumps, and a cross-country move and it is still working great on the nightstand in their daughter's room. Best of all, they don't worry about little fingers getting burned trying to turn the switch off. They think this may have been the best $4 they ever invested!

CFLs are intended to last five to six years and most come with a warranty. If the bulbs burn out before that warranty is up,

consumers can simply return them to the store where they made
the purchase, for an exchange.

A Word of Caution

CFLs contain about five milligrams of mercury
(much less than old glass thermometers, which
held around five hundred milligrams each). Though
CFLs contain only a small amount, mercury is dangerous. The CFLs do not release mercury when in use but
if a bulb is broken, the room should be immediately
ventilated by opening a nearby window, and gloves
should be used for cleanup. Never, ever vacuum a mercury spill. CFLs should also be disposed of at a proper
facility when their useful life is over. Visit www.epa.gov
or www.earth911.org for more details about proper
cleanup and disposal of mercury and CFL bulbs.

Investment #2

Unplug appliances when not in use = $0
Five-year return: $600 ($120 a year)

Nearly all electronic devices continue to pull a small amount
of energy even after the power switch is turned off. Some things
have visible or internal clocks, rechargeable battery backups, and
indicator lights. It's really hard to know if something is truly off.
The biggest energy drains we found in our homes were things we
had multiples of: cable and satellite boxes, televisions, video game
consoles, computers, and microwaves.

I never knew that having everything plugged in was costing
me money. I just assumed that if something was off it wasn't
using any energy. When I learned about this I ran around

my house unplugging everything I could find. What an easy
way to save money!

—Mary

Unplugging everything in our homes seemed kind of crazy and
time-consuming at first but once we got used to it, it was just like
any other habit. It settled right in. The trick to making this easy
was to put as many components and appliances on power strips as
we could. We thought about which items really needed to be on
even when they weren't actively being used. In our homes there
were only two, the cordless telephones and the DVRs (without the
DVR we'd never get to see a show from start to finish!). Everything
else went on power strips; rather than turning each item off separately, we flip the power strip switch and walk away.

```
--------------------------------------------------
            Don't Repeat Our Mistake
        We used to plug our cell phones in to get a full
        charge at bedtime and leave them plugged in all
    night. However, most cell phones only need an hour to
    fully charge. So for the remaining nine or ten hours we
    were wasting energy.
--------------------------------------------------
```

Investment #3

Hang-dry two loads of laundry a week (outside or inside) = $40
Five-year return: $360 ($72 a year)

The investment amount is for the clothesline and poles and
clothespins, or you can get inventive and make your own for free.

We aren't too crazy about the wrinkles that remain in our
jeans and shirts (especially cotton), so those items usually end
up in the dryer even if it's just for a few minutes to "fluff" them.

But hang-drying is a perfect way to dry sheets and towels, as well as undergarments and delicates. A complaint often voiced about hang-drying is that the clothing dries a little stiff. We were able to fix this by simply adding a cup of white vinegar to the wash.

Investment #4

Insulate water heater = $20
Five-year return: $240 ($48 a year)

Insulating our water heaters was very simple. The idea behind it is that a water heater that's not well insulated will allow the hot water it's holding to cool as it sits waiting for us to use it. It then has to heat the water a second time, wasting energy. New water heaters are usually already insulated but older models may need some extra insulation to help the tank hold the heat in. Insulation is measured in "R-values." It's important to find out if your water heater actually needs insulation by simply checking the heater for its rating. If the rating is at least R-24, it doesn't need any additional insulation. Kristin's was a much older model and didn't even have an R-value listed. In this case, the general rule is if the tank feels warm or hot to the touch it should be insulated. An insulating blanket and some duct tape is all that is needed. The blankets come precut and have instructions to follow closely to avoid damaging the water heater. Insulating our water heaters has saved us about 10% on our gas bills every month!

Investment #5

Wash laundry in cold water = $0
Five-year return: $350 ($70 a year)

We were surprised to find out that up to 90% of the cost of running a washing machine can come from heating the water alone. Most clothing stains are more likely to come out in a cold-water wash (the exception is oily stains) and hot water actually degrades colors and materials faster. On the flip side, it is important to wash bedding in hot water (note that the water needs to be at least 130 degrees Fahrenheit in order to kill allergens like dust mites). We wash all of our other clothing in cold water (using our homemade laundry detergent) with no concerns. Chrissy was astonished that using cold water got out spaghetti, chocolate, and even jelly stains better than hot water.

Investment #6

Adjust the thermostat = $0
Five-year return: $900 ($180 a year)

Each degree of change in your thermostat setting will result in 3%–7% savings on your electric bill. When we tried this we started with a goal to adjust our family's "comfortable" setting by two degrees year-round. This meant we were going in the summer from 76 degrees to 78 degrees and in the winter from 70 degrees to 68 degrees. These seemed like big changes at the time but we eased our families into it, and now we've achieved even greater savings. We only adjusted the temperature up or down one degree at a time. We would leave it at that setting for a few weeks and when everyone was comfortable (i.e., we heard no more complaining about being hot or cold) we adjusted it another degree. Kristin found that a programmable thermostat helped her family stick to their goal so they didn't have to think about it. A programmable thermostat can be purchased for as little as $45 and is very simple to install for someone with a little knowledge of home repair (find a friend, family member, or neighbor to help). Installing a programmable thermostat also helped us save more by allowing greater control over the daytime temperatures in our homes while we were away at work or events or on vacation. We simply set the program to adjust the temperature four degrees warmer (in the summer) or cooler (in the winter) when we'd be away from home for an extended period, and we also set it to start to cool or warm the house back to our desired temperature about thirty minutes before we would be arriving home. The important thing here is to not set it to vary the temperature too much. Doing so will result in your heating or cooling system working that much harder to recool or reheat the house. The Energy Star program recommends a seven-degree change during the day when the house is empty and a four-degree variance overnight when everyone is sleeping. For our families even just four degrees during the day was enough to achieve significant savings and still keep our homes comfortable for our arrival.

Don't Repeat Our Mistake

Be sure you understand how your electric company bills before you set your thermostat. When Kristin's family moved to Arizona in the middle of July, they settled in and set the thermostat on a conservative 79 degrees. That was a full degree higher than the setting they were accustomed to in Missouri. When their first electric bill arrived the following month, they were in shock. It was $400! Kristin had incorrectly assumed 79 degrees in Arizona would cost the same as 79 degrees in Missouri. She overlooked the extra charges during peak and off-peak hours and now realizes the impact one degree can have.

Investment #7

Seal cracks and leaks around doors and windows = $10
Five-year return: $400 ($80 a year)

We used caulk, spray foam, and weather stripping to fill energy-draining gaps around our house. These areas included door and window framing, leaks at the foundation (specifically in Kristin's home, which was built in the 1980s), holes where cooling system lines enter the home, and the place where the roof meets the exterior walls. These collectively are the equivalent of a three-by-three-foot hole in the side of our homes, allowing significant energy loss and wasted money.

Investment #8

Install a low-flow showerhead = $10–$60
Five-year return: $475 ($95 a year)

Low-flow showerheads reduce the amount of water used during a typical shower. A low-flow showerhead only uses two gallons of water per minute while a conventional showerhead can use close to four gallons per minute. It's easy to test your showerhead to see if this is an investment that would help your family. We placed a bucket marked at the one-gallon mark (just fill an empty gallon jug, pour all the water into the bucket, and mark a line at the water level) under our showerhead. We then turned on the water and made sure we were collecting all the water. We started a timer and let the bucket fill. We stopped the timer when the water in the bucket reached the one-gallon mark. Chrissy's bucket filled in exactly thirty seconds, so she opted not to install a low-flow showerhead; but Kristin's bucket filled in about twenty seconds (a rate of three gallons per minute).

Investment #9

Switch to low-flow toilets = $0
Five-year return: $125 ($25 a year)

We did not buy new toilets . . . we have an easier way. We simply filled up some of the space in our toilet tanks to lessen the amount of water used for each flush. A half-gallon milk jug works well for this. We filled ours with water, sealed the lid, lifted the chain in our tank to drain some of the water out, and set our jug inside. The next time the toilet was flushed, violà, we had a low-flow toilet!

Total investment: $150–$200
Total five-year return: $5,150 ($1,030 a year)

The investments listed above are basic home maintenance tips that require little money and are suitable for even the very inexperienced do-it-yourselfer. We managed these things with little help from family or friends. Kristin did make her husband install the thermostat and climb the ladder outside to seal up the house!

Even after we made all of these changes, we are still finding ways to save on energy costs.

In the winter, we open the blinds and curtains to help the heater out a little. The bright morning and afternoon sun is a great way to warm up any room of the house (and it puts everyone in a good mood!). Likewise, in the summer we are sure to close up the curtains and blinds around midmorning when it starts to get hot outside. Thermal drapes were one of our wisest choices for our south- and west-facing windows in the summer months (light-blocking or lined curtains are other options). Thermal drapes can cut your utility bill by 15%–25%. Chrissy has tons of windows on the south side of her home and the sun just beats down on the house because they only have two small trees in their backyard. She noticed a huge difference in the summer when she started closing all the blinds and curtains on the south side by midmorning and using blackout curtains. Blackout curtains can cost anywhere from $25 to over $100. Chrissy's mom helped out by taking her current curtains and sewing in a blackout lining. This only cost $10 for all her curtains!

We make sure to flip the direction switch of our ceiling fans based on the season. In the winter, the fans turn in a clockwise direction to pull air up; in the summer the fans are set in the counterclockwise direction to push air down. In the spring and early summer months, and again at the end of summer, using a whole-house (or attic) fan is a great way to cool your home while using much less energy.

Appliances around the house generate a lot of heat, so during the summer months, we restrict their use to early mornings or late evenings and sometimes even overnight. We run our dishwashers and washing machines during these cooler hours and try to avoid the stove altogether. If we do use the stove we try to plan some bulk cooking to make it as energy (and time) efficient as possible (see chapter 6 on kitchen and cooking tips for more details). Crock-Pots, toaster ovens, and microwaves are all great energy-saving alternatives to make use of during the summer heat!

Even though we restrict dishwasher use to certain times of the day, we do use them. They consume only about 20% of the water that is required to wash dishes by hand. Be sure to avoid the hotter temperature or longer wash settings and try letting the dishes air-dry. It takes a bit longer but when we run the dishwasher overnight, the dishes are usually dry by morning. However, if you really like washing dishes, that's a money saver, too! For some families, the cost of the electricity to run the dishwasher is more than the extra water.

Proper refrigerator storage and maintenance is another great way to save on energy costs. We talked a bit about the best ways to organize food in our refrigerators for efficiency in chapter 6. Refrigerators are estimated to be responsible for up to 15% of your home energy bill.[1] The refrigerator temperature should be set at 37–40 degrees Fahrenheit and the freezer should be at or below 5 degrees Fahrenheit. We make sure to cover leftover foods to minimize moisture buildup and allow hot foods to cool before storing them in the refrigerator; this keeps the compressor from working harder to keep the internal temperature correct. Since freezers actually work better when they have frozen foods in them (it's easier to freeze foods than it is to cool air because foods absorb and hold on to the cold) we keep our freezers about three-quarters full. We also clean our refrigerator condenser coils (these are located on the back or underneath the refrigerator) two times a year by vacuuming them carefully with our vacuum attachments.

This is not intended to be a complete list of steps that we could take and we're sure to find more. But it's a great place to start. Once you implement these things in your own home, we bet you'll find more, too!

Action Plan

1. Call your utility companies to inquire about their rates.
   a. Ask about peak seasons, peak hours, and special usage rates (such as billing more for the first 500 kWh and less for subsequent usage).
   b. Ask about special payment programs to help cut and manage your utility payments.
2. Pick three projects from the investment plan to complete in your home.

---

1   Reliant Energy (www.reliant.com/en_US/Page/Shop/Public/esc_topics_al _refrigfreez_home_shp_jsp).

3. Begin saving your utility bills to chart your progress. Your current bills will usually show a comparison of the current month's usage against the same month in the previous year. Pay attention to that and see if your bill is consistently lower.

4. Check BeCentsable.net for:

   a. A how-to article on installing a blanket for your water heater.

   b. A how-to article on sealing up air leaks.

9

Budget Breakdowns and How to Avoid Them

After all of our mandatory expenses (shelter, food, and utilities) are paid, we're still left with a huge category of spending that can quickly get out of control. This includes things like clothing, shoes, linens, household goods, pet care, auto and home maintenance, entertainment, and vacations. What makes this category even more difficult to control is the fact that these things tend to catch us by surprise. *Wow! Bobby's shoes are too small . . . he's growing like a weed. . . . Oh, no, the kids pulled the blinds off the wall!* or *It's July already? My sister's birthday is in a week and I don't have a gift.*

These are mostly things we know we'll have to buy someday, but there's no certainty in the purchase, so we fail to prepare for it until it's unavoidable. We know Bobby will need new shoes but we wait until he just can't fit the other ones any longer, then we run out to buy them, thinking all along, *I hadn't planned on spending $50 on a new pair of shoes this week!* In other instances, we are genuinely surprised by the purchase. How are we supposed to foresee our children hanging from the blinds pretending to be Spider-Man?

It's a recipe for disaster: we're "surprised" by the purchase, there's no budgeted expectation associated with it, and we are overwhelmed with the choices we have (which store to shop at, what style, what brand, which fabric, which options or features). As a result, when we go to make the purchase, we haven't put a lot of time into planning and looking for a great deal.

Right, but what can we do to avoid these things? Well, we have a plan! We can make a few assumptions and avoid a budget breakdown simply by planning for the things we can be sure will happen someday, as a result, making the true surprises easier to manage.

Here's How We Did It

We needed to really get the full picture of where our money was going in order to plan better. We made a list of all of the expected and unexpected expenses we could remember having over the past year that inevitably put us over our budget.

- Clothing and shoes (for everyone in the family)
- Baby and kids' gear and accessories (bags, backpacks, bikes, strollers, potty chairs, car seats, high chairs, etc.)
- Pet care and medicines (vet visits, heartworm prevention, flea and tick prevention, grooming, prescribed medications, training, day care—but not food or treats)
- Household expenses (replacing appliances, routine maintenance and repairs, decorating, lightbulbs, air filters, and even yard care)
- Auto maintenance and repairs

- Gifts (birthdays, Mother's and Father's Day, Valentine's Day, graduations, anniversaries, baby and wedding showers, etc.)
- Holiday gifts
- Entertainment (includes dining, attractions, and movies)
- Travel (all expenses related to travel)

Next we detailed the expenses for each category (Kristin finds it immensely helpful to use budgeting software to track her expenses from week to week) and how often they occurred (e.g., every other month, once a quarter, twice a year). Some individual categories may be a smaller or larger chunk of your family's budget.

Here is an example from Kristin's list and the detailed information she included:

PET CARE

- Vet visits: two dogs
  - Two general checkups = $100
  - One visit each year for illness or injury = average of $400
- Medications
  - Flea and tick preventative = $70
  - Heartworm preventative = $85
- Grooming
  - Twice a year for each dog = $140
- Misc. toys, new leashes, or collars = $45

In Kristin's example she has accounted for all of the care and supplies her dogs may need throughout the year and even includes expenses for unexpected injury or illness. She knows from experience that there is bound to be a surprise vet visit every year. When her family was in the midst of packing for their cross-country move, one of their dogs tore her abdomen open jumping their fence. It was late on a Saturday night and the injury required emergency care and several prescription medicines. That unexpected expense amounted to $750: money they had been planning to use on the drive to their new home. Kristin did not assume that full expense in her detail above because she knows that was a rare circumstance. She did, however, look at the previous three years and recalled at least one of their dogs needed unexpected care for an injury or illness every year. She simply averaged all of those expenses to come up with their expected expenses.

We detailed each category our family had (or could expect to have) expenses in, in the same manner.

Some Categories Need Special Attention and Extra Planning

We found that clothing, shoes, kids' equipment, and holiday gift giving required more planning. We had to spend more time in these areas, but the results were profound.

Budgeting for clothing, shoes, equipment, and accessories, for example, requires some forethought. It's hard to know when we will need new shoes (note we didn't say "want"—we always want new shoes!), but we can look back at our expenses to see what's happened in the past and use that to guide us in the future.

We have found it easier to make lists for each season, which also helps us plan for sales we know occur twice a year.

1. We create a list for each person in the house and start by taking inventory of what they have that can be used again.
   - Include hand-me-downs and last year's clothing that may still fit (or could be easily altered to fit).
2. Next we make a list of what we think each person needs (this is the hardest part).

- We consider the time of year, the typical activities we engage in during that season (special sports activities or performances requiring a specific type of clothing), and how often we plan to do laundry (an important consideration!).

Below is an example of what we wanted each person in our family to have for summer:

- 5 complete casual outfits (mix-and-match)
- 2 dressy outfits
- 2 sets of play clothes (kids)
- 3 pairs of pajamas (kids)
- 1 swimsuit or pair of swim trunks
- 2 pairs of sandals (kids)
- 1 pair of tennis shoes (kids)

Other upcoming purchases to consider are expensive items such as eyeglasses, strollers, bicycles, high chairs, and car seats.

Making a list of all our family's potential expenses really helped us see where our money was going. I found that making a list helped to determine what I really needed and what I wanted. Determining how much money our family needed was difficult to face but necessary to help us cut our budget!

—Holly

The other category we devote more time to is holiday gift giving, which tends to throw a large wrench in our budget every year. We always get caught up in the "spirit of giving" and overspend. To combat this we take extra time going over our holiday budget and we check up on it at several points throughout the year. We find it helpful to start our holiday spending plan right after the holidays, so our memory is clearer and we have as much time as possible to save.

Here's how we do it:

1. Make a list of each person we give gifts to each year.
   - This is broken into groups:
       Those we will buy for without question
       Those we hope to buy a gift for
       Those we may give a small "stocking stuffer" or card to
   - We then compare how much we spent the previous year and how our budget looks for the coming year to make adjustments if necessary.
   - Finally, we set some guidelines for each of the groups of individuals we hope to buy gifts for. Such as:
       Number of gifts
       Amount per person
       Even whether we should try to give only homemade items as gifts

One year Kristin's family decided to make homemade gifts for each other. It was much less expensive, the gifts took true thought and consideration, and everyone enjoyed the adventure of making and receiving something truly unique and made just for them! This is a hard task, we know that. It's not about deciding who gets a bigger or better gift, it's about making sure your goals are achieved. Buying gifts for children is more expensive because we are often buying toys or clothing, which are more costly per item. By comparison, we may be able to spend an afternoon making a very personal and special gift for our mother that costs very little but has as much meaning as anything we could buy at a store.

2. Next we make a list of all of the "extras" that pop up over the holidays and approximately how much money we spent the previous year, making adjustments for things we expect to change.
   - Donations

- Special-event clothing
- Holiday dinners and parties
- Special holiday activities or out-of-town trips
- Cards and photos (it cost us $25 just for postage last year!)
- Wrapping supplies
- Decorations

The total of all of this goes to our holiday spending budget line. It's likely that you will be surprised by this amount. We certainly were when we did it! When Chrissy sat down and figured how much they typically spent on Christmas and made a list of everyone they buy for, she was amazed. Chrissy and her siblings decided that the family was growing so quickly they would just start buying for the kids and their parents.

$ **Centsable Tip** $

In some categories we found we were consistently forgetting an important expense, like Grandma's birthday or souvenir money for traveling. To help with this, we started adding a little extra (about 10%) to the totals we calculated for those overlooked expenses. Sometimes we've not had to use it but when we did, we were thankful for the extra!

Preparing Your Life Raft

Once we've accounted for all of the extra spending, we need to start setting that money aside early. We know we are going to need it, so there's no point ignoring it.

After going through all of our extra spending, we need to

determine how much to set aside each month. How you go about doing this will largely depend on how disciplined you are about saving money for its intended use and whether or not you have expenses that occur throughout the year or at a specific time each year (such as birthday gifts and vehicle licensing fees). Chrissy can put everything into one savings account and know what every dollar is for. Kristin needs a more structured way to save her money. As a result, Kristin separates her planned holiday expenses when calculating how much to save each month.

Generally Chrissy totals her estimated expenses and divides by twelve months to find out how much additional money her family should set aside each month for miscellaneous or unexpected expenses. Kristin comes up with two figures for saving each month: one for her holiday spending, which is divided by eleven months, and one for everything else, divided by twelve months.

$ **Centsable Tip** $

We aren't always planning a year ahead for expenses. Sometimes we may start planning and saving for vacation only four or six months in advance. In this case, that estimated expense needs to be divided by the number of months left to save for it.

The Value of Time

It's hard to spend so much time planning for miscellaneous expenses that are still months away or may not even happen, especially when there are so many other places for our money to be going. Again, we agree, but it's the results that keep us on track.

This plan had a snowball effect on our budgets. Once we established that miscellaneous expense fund, we were able to better manage the amount of money going out and even save more than we could have without it. Here's how:

1. Having additional funds available specifically for the miscellaneous things that come up gives us flexibility to shop early to take advantage of sales all year and avoid being surprised by unexpected purchases.

    When we see a great deal on something we can grab it because the extra money is already there waiting for the purchase. For example, Kristin was able to purchase new shoes for her son and daughter at a big discount even though both pairs were about two sizes too big. Buying for the future was no problem and didn't put a dent in her budget because she had set aside money for clothing and shoes in advance. The purchase saved her more than 50% off the regular price and didn't interfere with anything they needed right away.

2. Big expenses are less stressful, giving us time to think about them rationally, make the best decision, and even enjoy them more!

    We were amazed at how much our holiday spending account helped us around Christmastime. We were able to sit back and enjoy all of the wonderful things about Christmas rather than run around looking for great deals and wondering if we'd have enough money to get everyone a gift. We knew we had set aside plenty of money and even had a list to help us remember every gift we planned to buy. Since we had the money available well before Christmas, whenever we found a good deal on the perfect gift for someone on our list, we were able to pick it up. We also avoided overpaying for items. Rather than waiting until two weeks before Christmas and paying whatever price was on the shelf, we were able to plan our purchases and take advantage of sales all year long.

3. Setting aside that money helps us get through financially difficult months.

We all have months when the income seems to be shrinking and our expenses are growing. Whether it's seven family birthdays in one month or something more unexpected like an injured puppy on a Saturday night, we've had them and discovered the immense relief of knowing there's a little extra savings.

It took us some time to start our different accounts, but once we did we discovered how valuable this budgeting tool could be! We used to stress every month about the gifts we had to buy and how we would fit them into our budget. With all the birthdays, and Christmas, weddings, and baby showers, it just seemed to never end. Now our family has a plan and no stress!

—Wanda and Joe

"I Need How Much?"

Once we gathered all of this information and totaled up our expenses our heads hurt! We were sure the calculator must be wrong because we just didn't have that much extra money to save each month. There was no doubt we were spending way too much and we never realized it until just then. It was stressful to see in black and white that, despite all of our efforts to save money on our monthly expenses, we were still wasting it in the most basic places.

Don't Repeat Our Mistake

Don't be discouraged! Don't assume the only solution is to cut out all of the fun stuff. This is an opportunity to make sure your family achieves the things that they value (like vacation time together) and eliminates the things they don't value as much (like five pairs of shoes). It's also an opportunity to think of more creative ways to get the things you need.

We began reevaluating our planned expenses. We went back to our lists to see where we could cut back. In some cases we cut out things altogether. Kristin's family made the decision to start making cookies and other treats for friends and neighbors and/or giving them the gift of time (an afternoon of help with a home improvement project or a day of babysitting so parents could have some time to themselves) for Christmas and birthday presents. In other cases the smaller budget encouraged us to challenge ourselves to do more with it. Chrissy's family cut their vacation budget but didn't change their plans at all. They challenged themselves to visit Walt Disney World for as little as possible and still have an amazing trip doing everything they wanted to do. They accomplished this by spending extra time planning and getting great deals on their lodging and transportation—saving over 50% in these two areas alone.

Sometimes having more money only leads us to spend it more easily. Our budgetary shock made us think about what we needed versus what we wanted, and then to value what we wanted against what we'd have to give up to get it. As a result, we discovered the forgotten arts of borrowing, bartering, and reusing. We thought of the hundreds of dollars we'd spent on things we only needed once or twice a year that were now sitting in our garage or in a storage closet taking up space and mocking us. Wouldn't it make more sense to borrow those items? We often borrow or swap special-occasion clothing and shoes between friends and family. It seems silly to buy a $20 pair of white shoes for our daughter that will only fit long enough to be worn for one event.

The Internet as a Resource for Free Stuff

There are several websites and groups created to facilitate community swaps or giveaways. Members list items they are not using any longer and in turn pick up things they do need. Community-based listings like those on Craigslist (www.craigslist.org), Freecycle (www.freecycle.org), and Freepeats (www.freepeats.org) are great resources. Sign-up is required to become a member and each community sets its own guidelines for activity. For example, one group may decide that members are required to list items for free before they are able to request or accept items from other members. The quality and selection of items from these resources is hit and miss. Strong community participation is a key element!

For those things we really need or just can't find anyone who can lend them to us, we've learned how to get great deals on them, too! In the next two chapters we'll share our tips for buying things in addition to groceries at rock-bottom prices.

Action Plan

1. Write down everything you spend money on that doesn't fall under the category of food, shelter, or utilities.

2. Pick out the three categories that account for the largest portion of these expenses.

3. Figure out how much your family needs for a full year of these expenses.

   a. How much did you spend last year?

   b. Is there anything new or unusual coming up this year?

   c. How many months do you have available for saving up for expenses like vacation or the holidays?

   d. Calculate a monthly figure.

4. Make adjustments if needed to bring the monthly figure down to an amount that will fit in your budget.

10

Discovering the Art of Resale

I magine if you could get a double jogging stroller for just $40 or a cappuccino machine for $50 (each regularly priced around $200). A new outfit or coat for $5 (at 95% off the regular price). . . . What about shoes or boots for half price? Well, you don't have to imagine, because it's real—we are doing it!

What's our secret?
We buy gently used. If you've never considered buying gently used or have considered it but had some uncertainties, this chapter is for you. We both love buying apparel and household goods gently used. It's not apparent by simply looking at our clothing or peeking in our homes, and only our pocketbooks know the difference (and we're pretty sure our wallets and purses aren't going to tell anyone)!

Our children have plenty of toys (which is to say too many), more than enough clothing, shoes that fit them properly, and as a result, they are always dressed nicely—in the morning at least; we can't control what they look like by noon after two meals, a snack, and painting! We have found less expensive ways to feed our shoe habits and to buy fun new kitchen and electronic gadgets, and even computers and designer clothing (when we feel the need!). You would never be able to tell the difference between our gently used things and the brand-new stuff our neighbor has.

> When I first found out I was pregnant I ran straight to the nearest baby store and got everything the "experts" said I would need. When my son arrived I made sure he had all the brand-new adorable outfits I could find. But after about six months I realized just how much our precious bundle of joy was costing us! I wised up and started looking for ways to get the cute things I loved without paying the high prices. I couldn't believe how much we save buying used and I am still getting all of the stylish things I paid full price for just a few months earlier . . . and no one is the wiser!
>
> —*Patty*

If you are one of the many shoppers wishing there was a way to save more and still be nicely outfitted but aren't sure this is the way to go, we think we can ease your fears! Keep reading. . . .

Does it take too much time?

Buying gently used can take more time if we aren't prepared and don't know where to start looking. We have to have a plan (it always comes back to that, doesn't it?). We have done our fair share of shopping for both new and used items and there are times when it seems inordinately difficult to find what we are looking for. Typically, the reason for this is we are simply looking in the wrong place. If we consider the best places to look for the item we are seeking, we can eliminate a lot of the time we would have spent driving from store to store and coming up empty-handed. One year, Kristin spent weeks looking for a quality, affordable Mickey Mouse Halloween costume for her son. Visiting store after store was disappointing and nothing fit the bill. She didn't want to pay $40 for a new one but she also didn't want to waste $15 to $20 on a thin, flimsy costume. A friend suggested she visit a local consignment store, where she finally found what she was looking for. She paid only $12 for a quality Disney Mickey Mouse costume, just a couple of days before Halloween. If she'd known where to look first, it wouldn't have taken so much time.

Aren't gently used items worn down and out of style—simply things that no one wants?

There are definitely some items in general that are not worth buying used. Some stores (often thrift stores) are more likely to sell very worn and out-of-date goods. Being aware of where to shop for specific items helps. The stores we choose are ones that make an effort to weed through these items. They buy and resell goods so they have an incentive to make sure the products are in style and in good condition. It is possible to find clothing and other goods in excellent condition at thrift stores and garage sales, too; it may just take more time. If you enjoy getting a great deal, this can be a fun way to spend a morning.

Changing Your Thinking

We believe the key is always to arm yourself with knowledge. If you learn some basic tips about shopping for gently used things, you will come out on top (with nice, new stuff and money in the bank!).

Used or New?

Before we rush out to buy something we need, it's important to think about the decision to buy new or used. Some things only require a split second of thought; undergarments, for example—definitely always new! Other things may require some investigation. This isn't a time-consuming task. It's likely something we already do anyway, we're just throwing in another option.

Is it safe to buy it used?

Certain groups of items just may not be good to buy used. Undergarments (as we've mentioned), personal care items, medications, safety restraint systems such as car seats and boosters, cribs, and breast pumps are on a short but important list of items it's really safer to buy new. Car seats and boosters are considered a hazard once they've been involved in an accident. The lightweight support and framing that is designed to protect your child can be compromised after an accident. Since the damage is not always visible and there is no way to know if a particular seat has been involved in an accident, it's best to buy new. Cribs and portable play yards need to meet specific guidelines for space between rails and the safety of mechanisms used to raise and lower the sides. Unless the make and model are imprinted on the crib and you are able to verify it has not been part of a recall, it's best to buy new. Breast pumps and the tubing they use can harbor bacteria if not properly maintained and cleaned. The bacteria can make both Mom and baby very ill; again, it's best to just buy new! Most everything else is simply a personal preference.

Will we save money if we buy it used?

The answer to this question is almost always yes. However, items that are in need of some minor repair could end up costing too much to be worthwhile. For example, Kristin purchased a very nice wood-frame stuffed toddler chair (the type you would find at a high-end children's store), secondhand, for her son and daughter for $40. The chair had a small tear in the upholstery. At the time, she thought it would be a simple fix. As it turned out, the proper repair would have added $25–$30 to the overall price of the chair. Her inexpensive, simple fix didn't hold and her children ended up making a giant pocket out of a small tear within just a couple of months. She probably would have been better off to buy a new one without the damage.

How long will we use it?

Buying gently used for children is typically wise because children seldom wear or use an item until it is worn out. Kids grow and their interests change by the day. Every parent can remember spending good money on an item that was worn once or twice or shoes that their kids outgrew in a week. Sometimes, they never even put these things on before they are outgrown. In our homes, toys are loved dearly for about a week, and then, unless our children are truly enthralled with them, shuffled aside only to see light again when a friend comes to visit. In general, children's clothing and shoes won't see more than a few months of use; books, movies, and toys could last for years or may be useful for only a few weeks. In our homes, we tend to assume very little for the children will be a long-lasting interest. We get books from the library or used bookstores and only buy new items when we just can't find what we're looking for anyplace else, or when we come across a deal so good it doesn't make sense to pass it up. If we know we have family or friends who can benefit from certain items we may opt for something new and pass it around to several families.

When we know we will get a lot of use out of something, we

will spend more to get a good-quality item. But quality doesn't always mean new. We have purchased many quality items used because we knew they'd still be in good condition or because we simply couldn't afford the new product. Some examples include articles of quality clothing, home goods (window treatments, linens, appliances, and decorative goods), electronics, and furniture. Certain things we are more likely to buy new because we know we will take good care of them or we'll get extended use out of them. A mountain bike, kayak, strollers, and car seats are great examples of items our families paid a lot for and have used extensively. Car seats have a five-year life span, meaning after five years it's recommended they be replaced due to changing safety requirements and deterioration. For both our families, five years was more than enough time for our two children to use the car seats, making our planned purchase of a quality product a good investment. Sturdy strollers are also a wise investment (whether new or used). We plan to continue using our strollers for several more years and then pass them along to someone else who needs one. We will cover how to buy new items at rock-bottom prices in the next chapter.

What to Look For

It's easy to overlook a problem with an item when we are sifting through hundreds of things and thinking about the amazing bargains we will find. Most secondhand and consignment stores only allow exchanges of items within a very short time period (e.g., seven days). For this reason, it is important to be extra diligent when making a decision to purchase an item. For toys, games, and miscellaneous goods we always check to make sure all of the pieces are present and the item does what it's supposed to do (or in the absence of instructions, what we think it should do). If it requires batteries and there are none in it, ask the store clerk to demonstrate for you. Most stores are required to check recall lists and remove recalled items from the shelves.

$ **Centsable Tip** $

It's always a good idea to check with the U.S. Consumer Product Safety Commission (www.cpsc.gov) when you arrive home with an item. If you find something you've purchased is part of a recall, simply print out the information and return it to the store for an exchange or refund.

When we are shopping for clothes we check seams and hems, look for holes or tears, and make sure the buttons and zippers work properly. A button may be easy to fix but a broken or missing zipper can be quite a pain for us, since we're not seamstresses. We also look carefully for stains or discoloration. For some clothing this may not matter but certainly if we are buying for a special occasion it will be very important.

Don't Repeat Our Mistake

We often got so excited about a great deal we would buy an item without giving it a good once- (or twice-) over. Later when it was time to wash and wear the item we would notice stains or discoloration or even a broken zipper. Our excitement had clouded our thoughts enough that we didn't check for these important things.

Where to Shop

Our favorite places to shop are at consignment sales events and stores. At times we may just want to save money. At other times we want to get more with our money, and shopping consignment frequently means we can get the things we really want without paying the outrageous prices. There is a significant difference between the two types of consignment; we will go over them separately.

Consignment sales events are where we get the most bang for our buck. At one children's sale, Chrissy found four Gymboree dresses in perfect shape for $5 total. Each of these dresses would have been $20 or more new at the store. Unbelievable! Kristin snagged a boy's down-filled Gap coat (again in perfect shape) for $20. The same coat was selling for $60 new at the store.

These types of sales are special events organized in communities across the country, usually twice a year (in the spring and fall); they strongly tend toward baby and children's clothing and equipment. Individuals sign up to sell their clothing (for a small fee) at the event and the public is able to shop. Several restrictions are placed on items for sale and each one is hand-inspected before being placed in the sale. These sales last for only one or two days, typically a Friday and Saturday. Prices vary wildly at these sales because each seller (consignor) is responsible for pricing her own items. But in general, shoppers save 50%–70% off the regular retail prices.

This is a great way to knock out all the shopping for each season at once because there are usually hundreds of consignors and so much space is needed the sales are typically held in a school or church gymnasium. When Kristin was expecting her daughter she bought everything she needed for a newborn at a spring consignment sale for just about $60—onesies, several summer outfits, blankets, hats, socks, sleep sacks, bibs, and even a high chair. The following year at another consignment event she purchased both her children's entire fall and winter wardrobes, including pajamas, Christmas outfits, Halloween costumes, coats, and shoes, for just $200!

Your first visit to a consignment sale will be eye-opening. Because the event lasts only a day or two at the most, and items are offered on a first-come, first-served basis, it can be a little crowded and fast paced! There are usually a lot of people and a long check-out line. On our first visit we were gazing in awe at the checkout line and wondering what could possibly be so wonderful. Two hours and a mountain of clothing later we knew!

While it's easy to find great deals at consignment sales, here are some tips to help new consignment event shoppers make the most of their trip.

First, know when to shop. The public is allowed to shop in a staggered fashion. Consignors and volunteers get to shop first; new and expecting moms are in the second wave; and the public is allowed in on the third wave. Based on what we are looking for, we may try to volunteer at the sale or wait until the last few hours—when everything goes to half price.

Shopping early is great when we have something specific on our list. Popular toys, furniture, and costumes tend to go first, so getting to them early is ideal. On the other hand, if we are just looking for a really great bargain but don't need anything specific, we'd wait until the last few hours and pop in to see what's left for half price.

Second, make some preparations. We have learned the hard way that we must arrange for child care if we expect to have any success. We give ourselves plenty of time (a couple of hours ideally, more if possible), and we have a list of what each child needs to get through the coming season and until the next sale.

The first time Kristin went to a sale she had her eighteen-month-old son with her. Rather than spending time looking over clothing and making sure she got what was on her list, she spent most of the time trying to keep her son from running in and out of the clothing racks and getting lost. She took lots of things home with her but many of the items were unnecessary purchases. There is also limited space in the sale. Many shoppers bring strollers or small carts to carry clothing around with them, and having a child in the stroller does not make this easy!

We spend a few days before the sale going through each child's clothing and shoes, trying on and weeding out the unusable items. We then make a list, by clothing type and size, of everything we feel our children will need for the next six months. At younger ages, this means we are buying several different sizes at once. We also measure our children's inseam for pants and jeans and their feet for shoes. If our children had long arms or were very tall for their ages we would take additional measurements. Even though items are sized at the sale, nearly all of them have been washed and dried. It's helpful to have a tape measure in our pockets so we can quickly measure these things to make sure they will fit properly. Remember, these sales are always final! If we overbuy or aren't checking the clothing closely we could end up with a whole closet full of really cute clothes our kids still can't wear.

> I went to my first consignment sale and got some fabulous deals! I can't believe how much money I saved. I will definitely return next time but I will make sure to have a list with me so I remember exactly what I need to get. When I got home I discovered all sorts of other things I needed and could have saved money on if I'd been prepared.
>
> —*Amy*

Third, know your plan of attack. Bring along a large (very large) tote bag or basket or stroller to carry things around in. The first time we went to a consignment sale we honestly had to stop to take a break because our arms hurt so badly from trying to hold everything. This goes right along with dressing comfortably. It's usually hot, with so many bodies in one space, and there aren't many places to sit, so comfortable shoes are a must.

When we arrive we hit the "hot" items first. These are the things that go fast: popular toys, furniture, baby gear and equipment, dress shoes, and costumes or other specialty clothing. Sometimes we can pay in advance, and the sale coordinators have SOLD tags they affix to these items; or sometimes they've specially designated an area for large or heavy items that we want to purchase but obviously cannot lug around with us. Once we've got this out of the way, we move on to the clothing.

For this part we use the "grab and go" method to save time and get a chance at the best selection. If we see something we think is cute we grab it and move on, no inspections at this point. We'll do that later. The reason for this is simple: if we leave it there it may be gone when we come back to it! We will keep looking until we physically cannot hold another item, then we find a spot to sort through and examine every item. We also check the tags. Each sale has its own tagging requirements but basically we are looking for a price and description that matches the item and to see that we have all the pieces that should be included. If an item has no tag or is tagged improperly, oftentimes the coordinator at the checkout will pull the item from the sale. It's best to just take care of this up front so there are no surprises.

Once we've examined everything and made our decisions, we replace the items we won't be purchasing and keep looking, if necessary, to fill in the gaps.

If the fervor of a consignment sale is not for you, there is an alternative: consignment stores.

Consignment stores are a great way to get some of the deals we find at consignment sales all year round, even for the adult members of the family. Consignment stores are owned by individuals who buy clothing from the public and resell it in their storefront. These stores are open year-round and keep a seasonal inventory on hand. Just as they do at the consignment sales, every item is hand-selected before it is purchased and placed on the rack, but consignment stores tend to be even a little more discerning because they want to be able to move inventory quickly. The environment is laid-back, there is no rush to get in and out, and most stores even have a small area where our children can play while we shop. The store selection is limited in comparison to a consignment sale, but we have the advantage of being able to shop any day of the year and to return to look for new things or even exchange items we purchased that didn't fit properly.

Some consignment stores offer discounts and coupons in local papers and to their members (through e-mail or direct-mail advertisements). Chrissy found a coupon in her local newspaper that said she could fill a bag with clothing for just $2. She got over ten items for that $2. This is a common promotion for these stores to offer toward the end of a season.

$ **Centsable Tip** $

When we are looking for something specific (maybe white dress shoes) it saves a lot of time to call ahead and ask the store if they have the specific item. If they have several, we can drop by to look at them. If they don't, we haven't wasted any time driving and looking around.

The growth of e-commerce has led to the creation of several **online resources** for buying and selling secondhand goods. Sites like eBay and Craigslist offer us alternatives to buying new or visiting local stores and garage sales by connecting us with people all around our communities and even across the country who may have what we are looking for at the right price. At eBay, an online auction site, shoppers bid on items that sellers around the world put on offer. Craigslist is an online classifieds site with listings grouped by metro area and various regions across the country and the world. Items (including cars and real estate) and services can be bought, sold, bartered, or given away and events and jobs are advertised.

Kristin started using eBay to purchase some of her own clothing at amazing prices. She visits stores to window-shop and find the brand, style, and size she likes, then she comes home and shops for it on eBay. She's purchased items made by Banana Republic, the Gap, and Tommy Bahama for less than half of what they cost in the store. Some of these items have even been new. She found a brand-new pair of her favorite running shoes (Mizunos) in her size on eBay for just $20, when they typically cost around $85. Now she buys all her kids' shoes on eBay—Stride Rite, Skechers, Crocs—all for half (or less than half) of retail. As we've mentioned, shoes are one of those things that children outgrow quickly. Most toddler and preschool shoes will last through two or three children before they are worn out. Every two to three months Kristin uses an online fitting guide to size her children's feet and looks on eBay for the shoes she wants to purchase. Usually with shipping, the shoes cost half (or less than half) what they would cost new—and sometimes, as we said, the shoes actually are new!

The key to bidding on auctions is to know what the item costs new so we don't overbid. We usually first find the items we are interested in at the auction and then do a search online for that same item or one nearly like it. Once we know what the regular retail price is, we can determine how much we are willing to pay for it. Second, we want to wait until the auction is just a few minutes from ending to bid. If we bid early we may drive the price of the item up too much. Bidding on items online is not entirely different from shopping at a consignment or garage sale. We can access pictures and a description and we are able to ask the seller questions about the item. If pictures are unavailable or the seller is using stock photos taken from a company website, it's up to the bidder to ask questions before bidding. Unless the seller has misstated some information or is lying outright, any misunderstandings in the transaction are the fault of the buyer. For this reason it is also a good idea to check the seller's return policy and other customers' feedback about the seller before bidding, to be sure they don't have any unresolved issues or consistent complaints.

Last but not least, we like to go back to basics by visiting good old **garage sales**! Most garage sale shoppers do it because they have patience and love the thrill of the hunt. Garage sales can be a gold mine or a complete bust. Recently Chrissy found a garage sale that was selling all the children's clothing for 25¢ apiece. She hit the jackpot picking up Gap, Old Navy, Tommy Hilfiger, and Gymboree clothes for her kids. Before we had children we visited garage sales frequently. Now, unless we can leave the kids at home with Dad or Grandma, we're on hiatus. We've found the best place to look for garage sales is in our community papers and on Craigslist. To be as efficient as possible when we do head out to garage sales we look for neighborhood- or citywide sales. We may spend a half day at these events but we are more likely to find the things we need and we only have to spend a couple of weekends looking. Be sure to get to garage sales early and take the cash you want to spend.

Reselling to Make Some Money

Even though we are focusing on ways to save money on purchases, it makes sense to talk about how things we already own but may not need or use any longer can be turned into cash to offset the cost of things we do need. As we mentioned, we buy most of our children's clothing, shoes, and toys gently used from consignment stores or sales or online. We can usually resell these items for as much as we paid for them and then use that money toward the next round of goodies. The lesson here is that buying gently used is a smart investment! For example, that Mickey Mouse costume Kristin searched high and low for (and finally found) would have cost $30–$40 new. Instead, she bought it used (which likely means it was worn only one evening, the prior year) for $12 and sold it for $15 the following year, a profit of $3. When Chrissy was expecting her first baby she was looking for ways to save money. She needed a bassinet for the baby to sleep in. Bassinets cost $75–$100 new and can be used only for a few months. Chrissy found a bassinet in almost new condition at a garage sale for just $25. She used it for both of her daughters, let her sister borrow it for her two daughters, and later lent it to a friend. After all of that she was able to sell it at her own garage sale recently for $20. A pretty good use of $5!

$ **Centsable Tip** $

We always purchase Halloween costumes and holiday dress clothing, including shoes, belts, and boys' blazers, secondhand or gently used. These things are almost never worn except on those special occasions. We buy them, wear them once, and sell them again the following year.

There are several different ways to sell our things. Each of the ways that we buy things used are also venues for selling our items. If we work backwards through the chapter we can see how the time involved lessens from garage sales (very time intensive) to consignment. Consignment stores are the least time intensive but we also get the lowest return here. Consignment sales events require a little more time (specifically, tagging and hanging clothing to meet the sale requirements) but earn more money as well. Auction sites and Craigslist are somewhat of an unknown. Generally if we spend more time taking pictures and crafting a good ad for our items, we will earn more money on the sale.

Whatever the venue, reselling items is a great way to offset the cost of buying the next round of things our families need. It helps clean out the clutter and save the environment, too!

Action Plan

1. Make a list of things your family needs for the upcoming season.
   a. Be sure to declutter as you do this: get a box or tub for outgrown or unwanted items.
   b. Make piles of what you will donate, what you want to sell, and what you must throw away, and do these things as soon as you are done.
2. Determine what your budget is (see chapter 9, on tallying and planning for household expenses, to make this easier).
3. Find out what your options are for both buying and selling.
   a. Visit BeCentsable.net for detailed articles on shopping consignment, auctions, classified ads, and garage sales.

b. Check www.kidsconsignmentsales.com for listings of consignment sales events nationwide.

    i. Visit the website of your local sale to note dates and read more about being a consignor.

c. Do a search for consignment stores in your area.

    i. Call to find out about their resale program.

11

Buying New at Rock Bottom

Like anyone else, we sometimes really enjoy that new, fresh-from-the-store feeling. There are times when we just can't find what we want secondhand or we don't want to buy it secondhand. Are we just destined to pay full price for some things? We think not! When we find ourselves faced with paying retail, we kick our centsabilities into high gear.

There is nothing like the feeling of walking out of a store with brand-spankin'-new stuff for a fraction of what everyone else is paying! With a little planning and research, saving money on new items can be just as easy as saving money on gently used items. Chrissy recently purchased $200 worth of clothing for just $50 and earned $10 in store credit for a future visit. Kristin bought $200 worth of dress clothes for her husband and earned $150 back in gas cards on a rebate!

All the tips and strategies we present in this chapter can be used to save money on anything new, even services like carpet cleaning. Once the basics are outlined, all it takes is a little creativity.

Use Coupons

Just as manufacturers distribute coupons for food and other consumable products, they often distribute coupons for durable goods; textiles such as clothing, shoes, and linens; accessories; and media such as books, DVDs, and CDs.

There are a few different types of coupons we look for based on where we are shopping. For in-store shopping we always visit the store website and look in the weekly sales ad for coupons either on a specific product or for some amount off our total purchase. We sometimes come across coupons for $25 off a $100 purchase. If that's more than we planned to spend, we ask our friends and family if there is anything they need or want. For Christmas one year, Kristin and her sister-in-law combined their purchases at a sporting goods store and saved $25 at the register. If we are planning to shop online, we search for advertised sales and specials at the store websites, then we look for "coupon codes" (online shopping's equivalent to a coupon) to save on shipping or to get discounts on specific products. Thankfully, there are a number of websites dedicated to finding, validating, and communicating these kinds of coupon codes. Our favorites are RetailMeNot.com (www.retailmenot.com) and FreeShipping.org (www.freeshipping.org). Coupon codes can also be found by simply searching the Internet directly; just enter the name of the store or brand and the word "coupon." For example, we could type "Gap coupon" in our search bar. This type of search will yield a wide variety of results that we must weed through, but if there are coupons available, this is one way to find them. We also find deals in coupon booklets (like the Entertainment book) and in magazines, flyers, and direct mail.

The Entertainment book is a coupon book full of discounts (lots of 50% off and two-for-one deals) for things we do every day: dining, attractions, retail, grocery, travel, and home goods. The books are printed for individual cities or regions and are available across the country; they usually cost $15–$40, based on the size of the area covered. The coupons are good for one year.

> I highly recommend buying an Entertainment book. It is without a doubt worth the money I paid for it! I read on BeCentsable.net that I could buy the current year's book at a deep discount in the spring when I reserved a copy of the following year's book in advance. What a great deal! My family had months to use the current book that I only paid a few dollars for and when the next edition was ready it was shipped right out to me. We used coupons for everything we could and saved hundreds!
>
> —*June*

Don't Repeat Our Mistake

Most of us receive a monthly mailer with local coupons (from companies like Valpak and Money Mailer) for dining, auto services, and even doctor and dentist visits. We used to just toss out these coupons without even looking at them. But it turns out it's always worth it to glance through them. There are usually a couple of really good offers and it's a great way to learn about new businesses in your area.

We also visit the website of every store we like in our area and sign up for their e-mail club or newsletter. This is a great way to get discounts and free stuff. We use that junk e-mail account we talked about in the first chapter to minimize the clutter in our personal e-mail account. Just set up a free e-mail account online with a service like Yahoo! Mail, Gmail, Hotmail, or your Internet service provider. Check it once a week or when you are planning a shopping trip or night out. You'll be surprised at what you find!

Shop Smart with Store Incentives

Most stores have **seasonal clearance** sales a couple of times a year and this is the perfect time to pick up some things off-season for yourself or something for the kids that may be too big now but will fit perfectly next year. You can expect to get season clearances for at least 50% off and sometimes up to 90%! We frequently pay attention to seasonal sales cycles to plan some of our purchases.

> $ **Centsable Tip** $
>
> Clothes, shoes, bags, and accessories will many times be on sale just before school starts and again in the spring.

Some stores offer another type of incentive where shoppers can earn **store credit** for purchases in increments of $10 or $20 and use it toward a purchase at a later date or even a specific time frame in the near future. Stores do this hoping to earn our money again and some even time this kind of offer with a seasonal clearance. They realize the clearance will bring in traffic they don't normally see and the store credit may get some of those people back. Two important things to check before leaving the store: 1) when can the credit be used and 2) are there any restrictions or exclusions on the purchase amount, or on clearance or sale items.

Price matching can be helpful for more than saving on grocery items. Refer to chapter 2 for more information on how to price-match. Our favorite thing to do on Black Friday (the day after Thanksgiving) is price-match! To save ourselves time and increase our chances of getting a really hot deal without standing in line for hours, we have taken ads to stores that will match their competitors' prices. We're really crafty and look for stores that are open twenty-four hours so we can get there early and wait inside out of the cold! One year Chrissy was able to price-match toys and movies for her kids and nieces and nephews, a digital picture frame for her grandma and grandpa, and a portable car DVD player and handheld digital video recorder. She saved over $400 and only had to visit one store to do it.

We continue to learn new secrets to save on things we never thought possible. We've mentioned that we both have dogs. We love them dearly but they do cost a lot of money! Vet visits, heartworm and flea and tick prevention, food, and grooming—and now that they are aging, there are additional medications—it adds up and for years this was one group of expenses we didn't think we could save on. Aside from finding a cheaper vet and groomer or cutting back on the quality of care we provide for them, we just accepted the expenses at face value. Slowly we started learning of ways to cut back. Specifically on the preventative medicines and prescriptions they needed. We discovered online sources for getting pet medications that were safe and reputable—and we discovered they price-match! Now we can search for discount medications from any site and ask the one we trust to match the lowest price. We have even found veterinarians who are willing to price-match the online sites. Doing this saves Chrissy's family 50% every month on their Lab's long-term maintenance prescription for severe arthritis.

Another great trick for saving money is to take advantage of stores that will accept **competitors' coupons**. Many national stores offer this incentive; all we have to do is ask. National home improvement, home goods, office, and craft stores are among the retailers now offering this incentive to their customers.

> I had been shopping at one of my favorite stores for years and never knew until I went to a BeCentsable workshop that they took competitor coupons! Now I watch the mail and newspapers for coupons from the other stores and use them to save money at my favorite store. I can't believe how long I've shopped at this store and never knew this policy existed!
>
> —Joyce

In recent years a secondary market for gift cards has grown and now there are several reputable resources for buying **discounted gift cards**. This is a great way to save some money right off the top, whether we are buying for ourselves or our family or giving them as gifts! We can buy these cards at auction, on gift card swap sites, or even in online classified listings. When we look for these cards we look for stores we've shopped at before and which we feel offer a good value. Check the details of the gift card listing and be sure you understand the fine print. Things to look for include an expiration date, a first-time use or dormancy fee, and restrictions on use in-store or online. Be sure not to overbuy! It doesn't help us to have $100 tied up on a gift card if we only need $50. The other $50 will be spent but maybe on something we didn't need. Also watch out for misleading offers like one we recently came across: a $500 airline voucher for just $300. The fine print revealed that the $500 was made up of twenty $25 certificates that could only be used one at a time on each leg of a trip. To make our $300 back, at the very least, we'd have to complete six round trips with that airline—and the vouchers expired just three months from the date of the auction! Another offer that seemed too convoluted and too good to be true. If we are ever in doubt, we tend to trust our instinct and look elsewhere.

> Discounted gift cards are an easy way to save money! Whenever I know I will be buying a big-ticket item I always buy a discounted gift card. We had plans to buy a flat-screen television last year and I knew we would be spending over $500. I went online and found a $500 discounted gift card for $400. We saved $100 and all it took was only twenty minutes online to find the gift card I needed!
>
> —John

Put It All Together!

In the first two chapters we talked about stacking coupons and incentives to save on groceries and other simple things. "Stacking" refers to using more than one strategy to get an item at a rock-bottom price. This same principle applies to everything else we buy, too! We've heard time and time again from our workshop attendees that they've just never thought of doing these things before. We know it takes some more planning time but the results are worth it. We love being able to buy our family things they really want, and we are able to do it because we think about the purchases in advance. We consider how to get them for less before we are standing in the checkout line. That's the key. Being familiar with your options is an important part of being able to plan ahead and save money easily.

Discounted Gift Cards and Rebates

Kristin knows she is going to need a new washing machine soon, so she has started collecting discounted gift cards. Kristin can combine these with rebate offers from two utility providers to save a good chunk of money. If she is really lucky, she'll come across a sale on the washer—wouldn't that be the icing on the cake?

KRISTIN IS STACKING TWO STRATEGIES:

1. Discounted gift cards
2. Rebates

Coupons and Sales

Chrissy needs a toaster. She got a coupon for 20% off her purchase in the mail recently. Then she remembered seeing an ad for a sale on toasters: $19.99 ($5 off). Bingo! To make this deal even better, if there's enough time before the sale and the coupon expires, she will look for a discounted gift card to use on the purchase. If she gets one, she will save 20% ($4) with the coupon plus $5 on the sale and another $5 from using the discounted gift card. That's an overall savings of $14. Pretty good for a few minutes of work on a toaster!

CHRISSY IS STACKING THREE STRATEGIES:

1. Coupon
2. Store sale
3. Discounted gift card

Competitors' Coupons and Sales

Kristin's family has taken advantage of competitor coupon acceptance policies to buy plants and other landscaping supplies for her home. One year the home improvement store near her was having a late-summer plant clearance sale. Because Kristin had signed up with another store's garden club, she frequently received coupons via e-mail; she knew that she could bring these competitor's coupons to the store that was having the clearance sale. By combining the great prices from one store with the competitor coupons, Kristin's family was able to get three beautiful hanging flower baskets for free. The baskets were on sale for $9.99 and her coupons were for $10 off any hanging basket!

KRISTIN STACKED TWO STRATEGIES:

1. Sale
2. Competitor's coupon

Clearance Sales and Store Credit

Chrissy wanted to advantage of an end-of-season clearance sale of 75% off to get clothes for herself and her husband. In addition, the department store was offering $10 in store credit for every $50 spent. She knew she would spend at least $50 so she bought a discounted gift card. She saved 75% on the clearance sale and another 10% by buying a discounted gift card, plus she earned $10 in store credit!

CHRISSY STACKED THREE STRATEGIES:

1. Seasonal clearance sale
2. Store credit
3. Discounted gift card

Coupon Codes and Sales

Using multiple coupons codes for saving while shopping online is possible; we just have to read the fine print. Typically coupon codes can only be use one at a time. There are exceptions, though. For example, Kristin purchased several items in a 70% off clearance sale at Victoria's Secret's website. She found a code for $5 off and a code for free shipping. She took advantage of this offer twice to buy clearance items. In the end she purchased three pairs of slippers and two undergarments for just $12 and some change.

KRISTIN STACKED TWO STRATEGIES:

1. Online coupon code
2. Sale

Price Matching and Coupon

We love to shop at craft stores, so when they have coupons available we gobble them up. Chrissy came across a coupon for $5 off a $20 purchase from one of our favorite craft stores. She held on to her coupon until the scrapbooking supplies she wanted were on sale for 50% off at a competing store. She price-matched the sale and used her coupon to get $40 worth of scrapbooking supplies for $15. That's more than a 50% savings.

CHRISSY STACKED TWO STRATEGIES:

1. Price matching
2. Coupon

General Guidelines for Stacking

The wording for a coupon code will specify if it can be used with specials offers, on clearance items, on shipping, or in conjunction with other coupon codes. In general, the policy that applies to goods purchased in-store is the same as the policy for online shopping: one coupon per item. If we have several different coupon codes for item discounts we can use as many coupons as we have items, but if the coupon states something like "20% off your purchase" we can only use one.

Coupons can be stacked with sale prices unless the coupon states "not valid on sale or clearance items."

Gift cards (even discounted gift cards) can be used in conjunction with any other offer. We think of these as cash to help lessen the confusion.

Price matching can be done even with a coupon in most cases.

It never hurts to try something; the worst thing that can happen is the store clerk or manager will tell you no. Don't be discouraged by being told no. We have been denied legitimate use of coupons and incentives because store personnel were unsure of the exact store policy. If we feel the offers we are redeeming are fair, we may ask to speak to a manager or call the corporate offices to clarify the store policies.

While some of these things may seem new and different, it does not mean you are doing anything dishonest. Remember, stores and manufacturers offer these specials, coupons, and incentives because they hope we will use them. They want to increase sales and get consumers to try and like their products. We are obliging and saving money for our families!

Action Plan

1. Check your favorite stores to see if they:
   a. Match competitors' prices.
   b. Accept competitors' coupons.

   c. Have any current coupon offers (ask where they can be found).

   d. Have a mailing or e-mail list you can join.

   e. Have regular specials offering store credit or steep discounts, such as seasonal clearance, "buy one, get one free," or "fill a bag" sales.

2. Try a simple stacking strategy.

   a. Combine a sale with a coupon at one of your favorite stores.

   b. Look online for sales and coupon codes to combine.

   c. Buy a discounted gift card and use it to purchase items on seasonal clearance.

3. Check out BeCentsable.net for:

   a. Resources to help you find coupons and coupon codes.

   b. Where to get your Entertainment book at the best price.

   c. Details about sales cycles.

12

Family Entertainment

Now a question everyone asks: what to do when you are lucky enough to spend time as a family but don't want to go broke doing it? Whether we're looking for a day of family fun or an evening of adult conversation, the game plan is the same. Budget carefully.

Everyone needs time to relax and get away from day-to-day responsibilities and worries. Time spent together as a family creates strong bonds and happy memories for everyone. By the same token, adult time is important as well. Having an opportunity to talk to someone who doesn't need us to change their diaper, wipe their nose, mediate a fight, or feed them is a great reminder that we (and our friends and spouses, too) have adult interests. Adult-only time helps us keep our relationships strong.

General Advice

We've talked about planning before, but it's time to beat that dead horse again. Planning ahead for entertainment can mean the difference between a fast-food drive-through and a five-star dinner!

A few general ideas for saving money on entertainment will get us thinking on the right track. We'll talk about those first, then we'll get into specifics about different types of entertainment.

1. Consider the time of day and day of the week carefully.

   Many restaurants offer special deals during their traditionally slower times and days. Likewise, most attractions will offer half-price or free admission on certain days of the week or during certain hours.

2. Use coupons.

   Coupons are also a great way to save on entertainment. "Buy one, get one free" offers from restaurants and sporting events are easy to find.

   Remember those coupon mailers we were tossing out? We found tons of coupons for local restaurants in every pack. We also can't stress enough the value that can be found in the Entertainment books. There are coupons, entertainment card offers, and special Entertainment.com deals that can only be accessed by members (either by owning a book or by paying a monthly fee to have access to the website).

   Another place to find coupons is online. When we find an entertainment venue or dining establishment we like, we go straight to its website to see if it offers any coupons. This is also the best way to hear about great deals at the last minute. Doing a simple online search for coupons will yield some new results as well. If you are looking for restaurant coupons just type "[your city]" and "restaurant coupons" into your browser search bar and see what comes up. Check the coupons carefully to be sure they are legitimate. We never pay for coupons or enter our personal information to get them unless we are sure we're on a legitimate coupon website or the restaurant's website.

3. Look for specials, promotions, and discounts.

Simply by signing up for a mailing or newsletter list we have received great offers for places we love to visit. Don't forget to ask about available discounts (student, military, senior citizen, or AAA). Kristin's family has come to appreciate their AAA membership for so much more than auto services (although those are pretty great). They often get discounts on family activities, dining, and travel included in their auto service coverage. Just show the card. Lots of establishments offer discounts to members of specific groups or clubs but don't outwardly advertise them.

4. Sign up for rewards programs.

Loyalty cards that accumulate points and rewards programs that offer us cash back are plentiful. Rewards programs are a great way to earn money back for visiting places our families enjoy anyway. A popular rewards program is Rewards Network (www.rewardsnetwork.com). You can also try searching online for "entertainment rewards programs" to find more.

5. Practice creative purchasing.

We have learned to never, ever assume full price is the only option. Consider purchasing in bulk, buying special discount cards, or looking for alternative places to buy tickets.

Always check to see if there are resale tickets available from an outside source like eBay or Craigslist (refer to chapter 10 for tips on bidding online). In states where reselling tickets is legal, there are plenty to choose from. There are also several websites, like StubHub (www.stubhub.com), where tickets are authenticated or guaranteed and auctioned to the highest bidder. When using these sites be sure to know what the face value of the tickets is, how the seller plans to deliver them, and that the site is reputable and offers buyer protection against fraudulent tickets. The site should have a Better Business Bureau (BBB) logo that links back to the company's BBB listing. We recently found NFL tickets for the upcoming season on clearance for just $9 each! If you live in an area that does not allow ticket scalping, it's likely you won't be able to find tickets on auction sites (like eBay and StubHub) or that the prices will be exactly the face value of the tickets.

Consider purchasing season passes for any activity your family does three or more times a year. It typically only requires three or four visits to recoup the cost of a membership, plus members get advance notice of other specials and often additional discounts and extra tickets for visiting friends and family.

Passes also give us a sense of flexibility. Chrissy buys her family a season pass to a local amusement and water park. This allows them to come and go as they please (or as the kids dictate) without feeling like they wasted money when they have to leave after thirty minutes because of an accident, illness, or temper tantrum. Kristin regularly purchases family passes good for a full year to family centers, museums, and zoos. She saves tons of money, and they always have something to do on a day when everyone needs to get out of the house but they haven't budgeted a $40 afternoon. As an added bonus, many of the passes get them discounts at similar locations across the country. For example, a zoo membership in one city will often give the card holder a discounted or even free ticket at a zoo in another city. Likewise for museums, science centers, etc. You can read more details about this in the following chapter on travel.

6. Avoid money traps.

Even once we arrive at our destination with discount tickets or coupons in hand, there are still a number of ways we might be surprised by unexpected expenses. Think of ways to avoid or at least lessen the cost of these "extras."

Avoiding money traps can be difficult when we don't know what they are or we haven't thought about them and taken steps to avoid them. Money traps are, in general, anything outside the main focus of the place, event, or attraction we are attending. For our families, money traps usually involve the kids in some way!

It's also wise to either carpool or take advantage of public transportation to and from a big event. It's likely to be safer anyway and may get you home more quickly. Many cities offer special rates and routes during major events. If you have the option, tailgate or picnic at the event. It's fun and inexpensive. Chrissy usually tries to plan a meal for before or after, using the tips from our meal-planning section to save money. Or have appetizers at home before leaving the house to tide you over.

7. Find an alternative.

Some months we really need to get away but our budget is already maxed out. In these cases, we turn to creativity to find a fun, free alternative to whatever our family is itching to do.

Check out your city's parenting magazine or website (these are usually part of national networks or owned and managed by the local newspaper or news channel), local newspaper website and associated blogs, and community or government websites like the parks and recreation department, chamber of commerce, or visitors' bureau. You'll find a great deal of events that are free or cost very little and learn about new things in your community as well.

These are the websites of some of our favorite national networks with local affiliates:

www.momslikeme.com

www.mycitymommy.com

www.todaysmama.com

http://gocitykids.parentsconnect.com

Many, many resources are not national; to find these simply do a Web search for [your city]" and "activity guide." You'll find great local resources and likely some national ones that we haven't come across.

8. Stack the savings!

Just as we've mentioned in previous chapters, we can combine several of these tips to save even more money. Try picking the slowest day of the week and using a coupon . . . or carpool to an event to cut parking fees, and then use a two-for-one admission coupon.

These general tips save money no matter what we are planning to do but there are more specific ways to save for each activity. In this chapter we'll share some examples of how we save on entertainment without cutting back on fun!

Movies

A classic night of entertainment at the movies has become so expensive that we now consider it a luxury. When we were young (like, so young our parents had to take us to the movies) tickets were just $3.75 each. We pay more for a soda now than an entire ticket used to cost. Kristin and her husband avoided movies for too many years. Two tickets and snacks from the convenience store ran a little over $20. Once they had kids, they could easily add another $20–$30 to the equation for a babysitter. Now that they've wised up, they have enough left in their entertainment budget to go out to two movies a month.

It's no secret that matinees are the less expensive showing, costing some $4 or $5 less per ticket. Some theaters have special ticket prices on certain nights of the week and nearly all theaters offer loyalty programs where moviegoers can earn rewards like free tickets and snacks.

It's nice to know we can still go to the big theaters to see movies when we want to, and we don't have to pay full price then either! It's easy to get discounted movie tickets. Here are five ways:

1. The Entertainment book has coupons, typically valid for up to four tickets, at a discounted rate (around 20%–30%).
2. Buy in bulk directly from the theater or through an agent (like www.bulktix.com).
3. Use AAA membership or other club membership. AAA offers a 30% discount on tickets in groups of ten to most national theater chains.
4. Buy discounted tickets from grocery stores and wholesale clubs (20%–30% off).
5. Buy a discounted gift card to a movie theater. See chapter 11 for details.

I am so excited! I just ordered movie tickets for 35% off the box office price! We had to buy several at once to get this great deal but decided to use some for gifts for my nieces and nephews. We saved money on entertainment our family loves and we have some Christmas gifts taken care of.

—*Carrie*

Now that we have the tickets for less, here's one of those opportunities for "extra" surprises to pop up and ruin our hard work. Now, we know theater snacks are overpriced, but they are delicious and convenient. Even here, though, there are ways to make these expensive treats a good value. For example, Kristin's local theater chain offers a loyalty cup that can be reused all year long to get drinks for just $1, and it offers a T-shirt that gets her family free popcorn all year, with free same-visit popcorn refills. These kinds of special deals make movie snacking affordable. When we do visit theaters without good concession deals, we bring our own. We either bring drinks from home or stop at a convenience store on the way to the theater to pick up a few snacks. They're much less expensive and they have a better selection. Check your theater's policy before bringing food and snacks from outside into the movie.

Movie Theater Alternatives

We aren't usually too concerned with seeing movies just as they come out and sometimes the big fancy theater in town is too crowded. This gives us an opportunity to go to the second-run theater. Traditionally this was called the "dollar" theater but with the rising price of entertainment, that's somewhat of a misnomer now. Still, the tickets are considerably less expensive, coming in at around $3 each, and we still get the feel of being at the movies. As a matter of fact, before they moved away, Kristin's family preferred visiting the second-run theater in their hometown. It was a hidden jewel, a historic restored theater from the 1930s, with just one screen, that was so plush inside they felt like they were in a luxury theater. Amazingly, the ticket price was $3 less than the state-of-the-art contemporary theater and much less crowded. The popcorn and drinks were even cheaper.

A great family alternative to the typical movie theater is a drive-in. Chrissy and her husband love to go the drive-in for a fun date night. The prices are low, typically charging by the carload rather than per person, and we can bring all the food we want; some places even let people barbecue! Drive-ins usually have a double feature every night. The two shows are geared for either family or adults so we can take our kids (who often fall asleep before the movies are over) to the family double feature and see two movies for the price of one. Truth be told, we really enjoy kids' movies! Drive-ins occasionally issue coupons or have special half-price nights. Check your local area for a drive-in.

Don't Repeat Our Mistake

Kristin and her husband learned the hard way that taking two toddlers to the theater requires too many snacks and trips to the bathroom to be enjoyable. They spent $35 on popcorn, Raisinettes, drinks, and movie tickets, only to make four bathroom trips and end up out the door before the movie was half over!

Kristin has now implemented a family movie night with rentals. Friday nights are "movie night," complete with pizza (homemade), popcorn, and ice cream. They typically rent one movie for the kids and one for the adults for after the kids are in bed. With movie rentals at all-time low prices and so many options (consider Netflix, Blockbuster Online, or Redbox) this is the perfect way to enjoy a fun "night out." An added bonus is that we don't waste money taking tired, cranky kids to the theater. Companies like Netflix and Blockbuster offer online movie rental plans for a monthly fee. Subscribers can create movie wish lists and have them sent directly via postal mail (and recently, even via computer). Redbox is the newest frugal movie rental resource. Redbox kiosks are located in fast-food restaurants, grocery stores, and drugstores across the country. Movies (even new releases) are just $1 for a twenty-four-hour rental. Even better, Redbox allows reservations, so when we go to get the movie we want, we know it will be waiting for us. Chrissy and her husband often get a free movie rental when Redbox offers free movie rental codes. These codes are easy to find online on a regular basis.

If paying for movies doesn't sound appealing, you're in luck! Many cities offer free movies weekly or monthly. The selection is usually limited to "family" movies but the events are free and open to the public; no reservations required. When we take in a free community movie we like to make a picnic out of it. We pack up dinner (maybe even our homemade pizza) and blankets along with some pillows and relax under the stars. We also take advantage of our tax dollars by checking out our local public library. Most libraries have a good selection of movies (on DVD and VHS) that can be checked out for a week or more for free. These films may not be the new releases but are likely to be fairly popular classics and recent hits.

Dining Out

Kristin and her husband love to eat out but one nice dinner can use up almost all their entertainment budget for a month. So rather than giving up their quiet dinners together, they got smart! Finding ways to save on dining is simpler than we expected. The first and easiest way to save is simply to change the time of day you go. Having lunch out is just as enjoyable as dinner and costs about half as much. Try taking advantage of lunch specials and you'll eat as well as everyone who will come at dinnertime and pay more.

Second, look for coupons! Coupons for dining are so prevalent it's funny more people don't use them. When Chrissy first started stretching her entertainment dollars she was stunned by how many restaurant coupons there were for some of their favorite places. They have also discovered some wonderful restaurants they wouldn't have tried without a coupon. Sunday and Wednesday newspapers are a great place to find restaurant coupons. Many sit-down restaurants offer coupons and discounts a few times a year as well.

Local newspaper and television station websites are some of the best resources for local specials and deals on dining (and a variety of other things). Also, an array of websites specialize in coupon codes, and a few even have special categories for online dining (e.g., ordering pizza)! We have also found discount cards and websites specific to our cities offering deals at local establishments. The discount cards are usually sold as fund-raisers by local schools and community groups. They are typically valid for one year and include twenty or more single-use offers.

> $ **Centsable Tip** $
>
> A great way to save money and celebrate our birthdays is to find out who offers free birthday meals. At some restaurants this requires us to sign up in advance, but for a free meal we don't mind at all! Who knew there were sites (like www.birthdayfreebies.com) whose resources are dedicated solely to finding birthday freebies?

When there is a restaurant we really want to visit but we are having no luck finding coupons, we check in with Restaurants.com to see if we can get a discounted certificate to use for dining. We can often buy a $25 or $50 dinner certificate for just $10–$15! Restrictions usually apply and they vary by restaurant but this is a great way to save a few dollars.

Make sure to sign up with a rewards program that offers points or cash back for every dollar spent on dining. There are also rewards programs such as the one offered by OpenTable (www.opentable.com) that offer points to diners for making online reservations (and keeping them, of course). When we know we are going to a restaurant that accepts reservations we take advantage of these programs to earn free meals as well.

> Who knew there were so many ways to save money on dining! I always assumed we had to pay the price on the menu. I can't believe how much money we're saving with just a bit of planning! Now my wife and I go out and enjoy dinner at much nicer restaurants, much more often.
>
> —*Eric*

Dining Money Traps

When dining out, money traps are anything other than the main meal. Appetizers, desserts, alcoholic and specialty drinks are all the items with the highest markup. It's best to avoid as many of these as possible. When Kristin and her husband have plans to go out for dinner they eat a snack at home before they go and make plans to pick up some gelato or a coffee on the way home. If they are still craving something sweet after the meal has settled, they have a good, inexpensive alternative (and probably use a coupon!).

Dining Alternatives

Look for the alternatives again! A special, quiet dinner at home is sometimes better than going out. Chrissy and her husband like to have a fondue dinner after their kids are in bed. It's less expensive, it's a special meal they don't eat every week (or even every month), they don't have to pay a babysitter or tip a server, and they can eat in their pj's if they wish. Kristin and her husband love dessert and wine. Since those are two items with the highest markups at a restaurant (they could account for 50% of a meal ticket) they like to do this at home. Even if they buy a premade dessert from their local pastry shop or bakery, it's considerably cheaper. We don't always feel like making our own special dinner but when we do, this is a winner!

Music and Theater

When booking symphony, opera, or theater tickets, consider going to the late afternoon show, which is likely to have fewer in attendance, or go to a rehearsal show. Many groups offer tickets to the public for rehearsal shows a few nights before the full event. These are almost always just as good as the advertised event and you may even get to see more behind-the-scenes activity. Ticket prices will be lower for these shows. Be sure to know the layout of the venue when selecting which tickets to purchase. Seating that's closer to the stage in a particular venue may not be worth the premium charge. Also check with your local radio or news station or even your employer for special offers.

$ **Centsable Tip** $

Stop by the box office just before the event starts to
see if there are tickets available at a discounted rate.
The event manager would rather sell the tickets at a
discount than have empty seats in the house.

Music and Theater Alternatives

Many cities offer free concert-in-the-park events or community
music and theater festivals that are free or at very low cost. These
events are a great opportunity to see several performers, making
them a good value for the money. We have also found these venues
to be the least restrictive about food and beverage. We've taken
picnic dinners and wine or even our portable grill and cook dinner
there.

Universities, community centers, and community theater
groups offer inexpensive and sometimes free plays, musicals, and
concerts. These are available year-round but more events are scheduled around the fall and winter holidays. If you live near a university you are likely to have a diverse mix of inexpensive events and
activities to choose from during the school year. Check out their
community events calendars online.

Sporting Events

Our husbands are big sports fans, but unfortunately tickets to
sporting events are expensive and sometimes hard to come by. The
best defense for high ticket prices is planning ahead and knowing
how to get the best price. First, consider the game you want to
attend. If demand for that game is expected to be higher, the team

will likely raise the ticket prices. This can be because of the time of year, holidays (when more people are off work and free to attend), or, of course, the popularity of the opponent or the team matchup. Second, look for alternative places to buy your tickets. Some teams, like the St. Louis Cardinals, help their season ticket holders sell tickets that they won't be able to use at a discount. Kristin bought her father, a lifelong St. Louis Cardinals fan, tickets to see a game in the new stadium for about 30% less than what they would have cost from the box office. Another benefit is that season ticket seats tend to be in good locations in the stadium or ballpark. Keep an eye out for game packages that get you ten tickets for the price of eight, or look for special events. Chrissy has frequently taken advantage of "Buck Night" offers at the baseball stadium in Kansas City—she could see a game for the price of a general admission ticket, and get food for a buck! Sometimes local shops and grocery stores pair up with the local sports team to offer discounted or free ticket vouchers with specified purchases.

Amusement and Water Parks

Timing is everything at amusement and water parks! Most parks offer special weekday and evening rates. If your schedule is flexible, going in the evening or on a weekday is a great way to save money (usually half the ticket price). Some parks offer even better specials at the open and close of a season. Chrissy was able to take advantage of two great offers at once to get half-price admission to a park for an evening and the following day for free! Her family turned this into a mini getaway one weekend, by driving three hours to a nearby city and buying half-price evening admission tickets to play before bed; the next day they got back in for free.

Coupons are pretty easy to find for amusement and water parks.

It's also a great idea to call the park and simply ask if there are any discounts or special offers available, such as redeeming soda cans or other product purchases for discounted tickets. Some parks offer loyalty programs like the movie theaters we mentioned earlier in the chapter.

> $ **Centsable Tip** $
>
> Watch out for the big money traps, such as food and drinks. If you will be getting a drink, be sure to buy a souvenir cup that includes free refills all day, sometimes even on future visits.

For an alternative to amusement parks, a visit to the state or county fair might be just the ticket (at a fraction of the cost). While these occur only once a year, they are chock-full of fun and activities for the whole family. Guess what? We can get coupons for these tickets, too! Many of the same places offering discounted sporting event tickets also offer discounted state fair tickets. Check the fair's website and your local newspapers and magazines as well.

Community Family Attractions: Zoos, Museums, and Family Centers

Community attractions are great because they are designed specifically for families and are meant to be low-cost, high-value entertainment that's also educational. They usually have plenty of bathrooms with child-friendly changing areas, plenty of kid-friendly activities and spaces as well as informal seating and picnicking areas, and lots of water. Finding discounts for these attractions follows the same guidelines as for all the other places:

look in the Entertainment book (or another local coupon book or card); look online; check their website for specials.

Your local library is one additional savings resource for this. Many libraries team up with their communities to promote local educational attractions. For example, Kristin's local libraries have a summer program that allows residents to check out free family passes to local attractions like the science center, museums, and the zoo. The pass is free for the user (you just need to have a library card) and doesn't have to be returned for a week. We've also seen coupons for "buy one, get one free" admission to these same attractions in our library's quarterly publications.

Once we've looked for deals to get the best price we can on admission, we only have to make it past all the money traps inside. Most family centers and zoos allow visitors to bring a cooler of food and drinks, plus a stroller or wagon, and never bat an eye. Visiting a museum is a great reason to picnic at a nearby park. Just be sure to find out any restrictions before leaving the house to avoid surprises (or disappointments).

Family Tips

Entertaining children is hard work! We love to take our kids to do fun, out-of-the-ordinary things. Visiting a museum, going to a movie, or attending a sporting event with kids can not only be exhausting but it can empty our wallets fast. Thankfully, there are some ways around this.

For example, during the summer months many movie theaters offer kids' movies for almost nothing. Kristin got passes for her kids and herself for eleven weeks of movies for just $10 each for the whole summer! That's less than a dollar a movie. In that case, she didn't mind taking two toddlers to the movie theater. If they weren't enjoying themselves they didn't feel bad leaving, because the price was so good!

Taking the kids out to lunch or dinner can be inexpensive, too, if we follow a few simple rules.

1. Find a restaurant that has a "kids eat free" program. There are literally hundreds. Visit www.kidseatfree.com to find your city and the restaurants you can visit.

2. Never, ever buy milk at the restaurant. It can cost as much as a gallon of milk costs at the store, and the kids probably won't drink it all. We always bring milk in sippy cups from home or just order water to drink.

3. Kids' meals are usually a good value but not always the healthiest foods. We've shared our own meals with our children and ordered things we knew they would eat à la carte from the regular menu. This works particularly well for kids with food allergies. Kristin's son has to avoid gluten and ordering à la carte gives them the flexibility of asking for special preparation or ensuring he's eating something "safe."

4. Pick the "right" place and bring some toys. Most kids like noisy, active places with fun things to look at, but they lose interest in them about five minutes after ordering. We bring crayons, paper, small puzzles, books, and cars with us to entertain the little ones. Chrissy and her family have found that buffets are great for families with young children because everyone can get their food first thing and everyone can find something they like and dessert is usually included.

Taking kids to sporting events can be great fun if the event is child friendly. Kristin and her husband bought tickets to a major-league baseball game when their two children were just one and three years old. They had a great time during the first forty-five minutes. The next hour was split between walking the kids around, finding snacks and drinks, and chasing them up and down the stairs (a rather dangerous activity for everyone!). Finally the grown-ups threw in the towel They missed half of the game, spent an extra $20 on food, and had two grumpy kids for the ride home. Needless to say, they haven't done that again! We have found that, generally speaking, college and minor-league events are more appropriate and entertaining for children. Minor-league teams tend to put on more of a "show" to keep guests returning to their games. Major-league teams are focused on the game and they know most of their fans are as well. Chrissy and her family have season tickets for college football. They have found college games are the perfect venue for the entire family and the kids love to tailgate before the game.

Stacking the Strategies to Save Even More

Now that we've outlined all the savings opportunities there are, we want to make sure to use them to the fullest advantage. Here's where stacking comes in again; it's always the same—we can stack one or more strategies to get the best possible price.

Here's how it works:

Kristin and her husband have finally planned a date for next weekend. The date is only seven days away, so Kristin gets busy planning. Their budget for the night is $75, including paying a babysitter.

Both Kristin and her husband really love a night at the movies and dinner at an Italian restaurant, and they have a weakness for wine and dessert when they go out. But the babysitter will cost $30, leaving Kristin with only $45 to spend. Kristin looks online and finds an Italian restaurant with good reviews. In a local area coupon book they purchased earlier in the year Kristin spots a coupon for "buy one, get one free entrée" at the restaurant. Although the coupon is only good until six p.m. on Saturdays, the timing is perfect for them. Kristin estimates that, with the coupon, dinner will cost about $20 with a tip. Using their AAA discount they are able to get movie tickets for just $6.50 each. With the remaining money left over from the budget, Kristin buys the ingredients to make a cheesecake.

On Friday, one day before date night, Kristin makes her home-made cheesecake with sliced strawberries. The total cost is $8 for the whole cheesecake, but she also could have bought two slices at a local bakery for about the same price.

It's Saturday, the big day! Kristin and her husband already have several bottles of wine on hand, so they just chill one so it's ready when they get home. They have a great dinner, head to a movie afterward, and even have money in their budget for a soda. They are sure to stay out long enough that the kids are in bed before they arrive home. After the babysitter leaves they enjoy their dessert and wine in lovely peace and quiet!

DATE NIGHT COSTS

$20 for dinner and tip

$13 for movie tickets

$2 for two sodas at the theater (using the loyalty cups we men-
    tioned earlier!)

$8 for cheesecake

Total for the night = $43 (plus $30 for the babysitter)

Without these planning and saving strategies, this night would have cost around $120. They saved over $40.

Action Plan

1. Think of the things you and your family like to do for entertainment on:
    a. Dates.
    b. Family days.
2. Using this chapter as a guide, look for two ways to save money on each activity.
3. Check out BeCentsable.net to see a list of resources we recommend for:
    a. Coupons.
    b. Rewards programs.
    c. Coupon books and discount cards.
    d. Tickets to events and attractions.
    e. Redbox free movie codes.

13

Travel

After all the effort and energy we put into saving money on day-to-day activities, we realized we could save money on anything. One of our families' favorite things to do is travel. Whether we are taking a mini road trip for a weekend or a ten-day vacation skiing, we enjoy the time together to break out of our daily routines and make great memories.

Our children are still small but they are so awestruck by the things they see: the ocean, mountains, snow skiing, Native American ruins. It gives us a chance to teach them about the rest of the world and helps them imagine new things.

Our families have very different traveling routines. Because of our husbands' work schedules, we each arrange different getaways that work best for us. Kristin's family is more apt to take a half dozen weekend road trips through the year while Chrissy's family takes longer but less frequent trips, usually lasting a week to ten days at a time.

What we've discovered, though, is that it really doesn't matter what type of vacation we want to take—we can save money and use it to cut our budget or to extend our vacation by a few days.

Planning

Planning vacations can be a lot of fun and sometimes a lot of headaches! We are always more motivated to plan ahead when we set out to cut our expenses. The Internet is the best tool at our disposal for traveling. From finding the best places to visit and tips for saving money to making reservations, we can do all of our travel planning in our homes, at the computer.

Even when we know exactly where we want to go and how we're going to get there, doing a little research can broaden our horizons. We come across attractions, events, and adventures we didn't know existed; we can find out about special hotel offers, airfare and car rental deals, and dining coupons just by reading a little on the Internet. A quick Internet search on a reputable website for coupon codes will save 10%–20% easily. Codes exist for hotel rooms, dining, car rentals, train or bus fare, attractions, event tickets, and shopping—all the same tips in the previous chapter on entertainment can be used to find deals for travel; we're just looking in a different city.

$ **Centsable Tip** $

For hotels and airfare or other transportation, be sure to check several options before determining which deal is the best one. Prices vary wildly and ads and descriptions can sometimes be misleading.

We recommend checking travel sites like TripAdvisor (www.tripadvisor.com), Lonely Planet (www.lonelyplanet.com), Smarter Travel (www.smartertravel.com), Frommer's (www.frommers.com), or Yahoo! Travel Guides (the list is long and there are dozens more; check our website for current links) for tips and advice from people who've been there and done it all. Each review site speaks to a different type of traveler. Read reviews from a few different sources to see who has tips most valuable to you.

Should We Book Early or Wait Until the Last Minute?

It's hard to decide sometimes if we should book our travel early or wait until the last minute. We find good deals on both sides. The decision usually becomes centered on how flexible our travel dates and times are. If we just want to take a trip sometime late in the summer, it might be a good idea to check on last minute deals two weeks before. If we know we only have specific days for vacation due to work schedules or need to ask for time off work in advance, it's a better idea to plan further ahead in the interest of having an enjoyable vacation within our time constraints.

Booking transportation and hotel rooms early means we get exactly what we want. Sometimes it will save us money. In general, air fares will increase as travel dates near. We don't have to worry about a hotel being booked and paying a higher rate for a room we don't need or staying somewhere that's not really what we wanted.

Sometimes booking at the last minute is worthwhile, too. We've gotten great last-minute travel deals booking within five or seven days of departure. Airfare may go down if there are several open seats on a flight because the airline makes increasingly more profit with each ticket sold. Fuel and overhead will essentially cost the same whether the plane is 50% or 100% booked. The airlines are willing to take less because they know they are making a higher profit selling the last few seats at a discount; likewise for hotels. Waiting to book a room a few nights before arrival can be risky but we may get a really great deal if the hotel isn't already sold out.

Kristin had to fly from Phoenix to Kansas City with only two weeks' notice. She took a gamble and waited until the last minute to book her airfare. She was able to book a nonstop flight with only a five-day advance purchase for just $160 round trip. Just a few weeks prior to that, the rates were around $300. By waiting until the last minute she saved nearly 50%. The plane was full, but so was her pocketbook!

When to Travel

Doing a little research first improves our odds of knowing when we see a great deal and of snagging it at the right time. We research the high and low season for vacation destinations. It's common to save 50% or more by traveling in the off-season; we gain time, too, since attractions and restaurants aren't nearly as crowded.

Research isn't necessary for all the travel that we do; sometimes it's pretty obvious when the popular season is for a given location and we may not be able to alter our travel dates. Often, though, we are surprised by what we discover. High and low seasons are determined by a number of factors that differ from region to region. The weather, school schedules, annual fairs, and holidays are all things that influence a particular area's high and low season. For example, one of Walt Disney World's off-seasons occurs just after Thanksgiving but its high season starts the week prior to Christmas and lasts through New Year's (because of the park's annual holiday event and the mild Florida weather). To get the best deals at Disney, Chrissy planned a trip for the first week of December. Since it's one of the slowest travel times of the year she was able to get plane tickets for $100 each (a nonstop flight) and a hotel for only $29 a night!

In Arizona, where Kristin's family lives, the off-season lasts all summer long. It's just too hot for most travelers to want to come during June, July, and August. That's great for her family because they can get awesome deals at hotels in nearby cities with water parks for half what it typically costs. That's the ultimate "staycation"!

> I was amazed at how much money we saved by traveling in a lower season. When we first started planning our trip we were going to vacation at the end of March. Once we did some research we found out this was a high season because of spring break. By moving our trip to just two weeks later we saved 10% on our hotel room alone!
>
> —Tom

Getting There—Things to Consider

One of the most costly travel decisions (and the one with the fewest alternatives) is transportation. Quite often, the cost of getting to our destination will help us decide right away if we can really afford the trip or not. There are many pros and cons to consider about choosing transportation methods. Ultimately it comes down to price and convenience. If the price fits in our budget and the convenience factor is high, we'll usually fly, but we sometimes overlook the hidden costs of choosing one method or the other.

For example, Kristin's extended family lives in Missouri. Each year she packs up the kids and makes the fourteen-hundred-mile trip across the desert back to the Midwest. Typically, Kristin makes this trip alone with her kids in their van. Her husband meets them for a few days, arriving by plane so he can make the most of his five days off work. But the decision for Kristin to drive or fly is one that they reconsider each time. Flying with two children would cost around $500–$600 since all three now need airline tickets (children age two and under fly free as a "lap child" with most airlines; and if the plane isn't full, they can snag a seat for free). Driving costs only $300 for gas round-trip but it also means that the family is on the road for thirty-six hours and has to pay for two nights in hotel rooms. We can see right there the cost is about the same. So how do they decide? In this case, it comes down to convenience. Kristin, traveling alone, can't manage handling two car seats, luggage, and two children who need constant supervision all at once in a busy airport. Also, if Kristin and her kids fly, the issues are compounded in Missouri because she has to figure out who can chauffeur them around town during their visit (considering, also, who has room for three extra people and two car seats in their vehicle). If Kristin flies and rents a vehicle, a few hundred dollars are added to the overall travel expenses.

So Kristin will keep driving, unless, of course, she can get three round-trip airline tickets for less than $400. That would equal the expenses of driving and also eliminate the hassle of spending three days stuck on the road with little ones!

General Money-Saving Tips for Air Travel

The most important thing to do when looking for great air travel deals is to compare prices from several different websites and airlines before booking your flights. Unless we have a voucher for *free* travel, we check every airline to make sure we aren't overpaying. There are a variety of factors that go into determining a ticket price and a variety of things to consider when looking for a good deal, such as layovers and connections. Typically, for the inconvenience, a flight with a layover or connection will cost less than a direct flight. (Not always, but typically.)

Select your travel dates and time strategically. Business travel flights during the week tend to have a little higher rate, as does travel spanning a weekend (Friday to a Sunday). To get better rates try shifting departure or arrival dates by one day. Traveling mid-week (for example, Wednesday to Tuesday) tends to be the least expensive. Avoid the three to four days before and after a major holiday. Travel (ground and air) peaks at this time and airlines charge a premium.

Avoid last-minute bookings if your dates and travel times are firm. On the other hand, if your travel is flexible and a nonstop flight isn't a necessity, last-minute booking could save you a considerable amount of money.

Where to Look for Unbelievable Airfare Deals

There are many sources for discounted airline tickets. Online travel sites are good at aggregating the best deals on the Web. Sites like Travelocity (www.travelocity.com), Orbitz (www.orbitz.com), and Cheapflights (www.cheapflights.com) will search major airlines to find the lowest rate on your travel dates and even make suggestions for getting a better deal (like flying into a smaller nearby airport or shifting travel dates).

We sign up to receive specials and newsletters from a few airlines we find value in. With these communications, we get advance notice of fare specials and other offers. In some cases, the airlines will drop fares on their website dramatically for a period of time. It's also important to keep in mind that some airlines don't submit their fares to the above-mentioned websites. These are usually smaller regional airlines only operating in the United States. Two good examples are Allegiant Air and Southwest Airlines. For this reason, it's a good idea to check the arrival and departure schedules or terminal listings at the relevant airports to see which airlines operate there, then visit each airline's website for special offers that may not be advertised in other places. We've discovered a great small airline, operating at a regional airport near us, that flies back to our hometown every week. We can get tickets for much less and we never would have found the discounts without some research.

$ **Centsable Tip** $

Remember to research high and low season at your destination and avoid holiday weeks. We've learned that, across the country, the lowest air travel season is the two weeks just after Thanksgiving. If our schedule is flexible, we'll travel then.

The best way to get a cheap airline ticket is through a bidding or auction site. Bidding on airline tickets is more like negotiating directly with the airline for its lowest price, versus what we see on eBay, where the price is bid up from a certain starting point based on demand. Airlines may accept or reject an offer and even make a counteroffer. Bidding on Priceline.com (www.priceline.com) can save up to 50% on airfare. Take note, however, that we do not get to choose our flight times, stops, connections, or airline preference when bidding. This is similar to a "blind" auction, meaning we don't see other bids and we don't know the details of the offer until it is accepted. We are able to dictate the airport and travel dates only.

We get started by researching the lowest fares we can find for our travel dates. Great sites to help with this are Airfarewatchdog .com (www.airfarewatchdog.com), Expedia (www.expedia.com), and FareCompare (www.farecompare.com). Once we see what the lowest ticket price is, we visit Priceline.com and bid on those same travel dates.

KEYS TO SUCCESSFUL BIDDING

1. Bid lower than 50% at first (remember, this doesn't include airline fees—which usually amount to some $50 per ticket).
   - For a flight that's running $200 round trip, we'd bid $75 first.
2. If your bid is not accepted, read the screen carefully for a counteroffer and note the amount and whether or not it includes fees (sometimes the counteroffer will include fees). We *don't* take the first counteroffer unless it's right at or close to 50% less than the best rates we found on our own.
3. Start over, but this time bid just under the counteroffer.
   - For the $200 ticket mentioned above, we bid $75 at first and Priceline.com countered with $150 (excluding fees); we bid again at $100.
4. Repeat this process until you see the lowest price available (in two or more duplicate counteroffers) or your bid is accepted!

Kristin was able to get round-trip tickets from Atlanta to Phoenix, selling for $430 each, for just $300 each doing this. The first counteroffer was $300 and did not include $50 in fees. The second counteroffer was for $300 (fees included). Score!

Renting a Car—Tips Before You Hit the Road

The decision to rent a car can come with some costly baggage if we don't do our research ahead of time. Rental cars often include extra fees and insurance and, of course, we still have to pay for fuel. But there are opportunities to save money if we look for them. For example, we found out that our own auto insurance covers the insurance for our rental cars (the person renting the car must be a driver insured on our policy) and that some car rental companies even cover the cost of tolls on toll roads.

Don't Repeat Our Mistake

Kristin and Chrissy have each traveled to cities with toll roads recently. The car rental company Kristin used did not cover tolls but the one Chrissy rented from had a toll pass in the vehicle. A little research would have saved Kristin an extra $20 and close to an hour of stops on her trip.

Making the decision to rent a car at all should be weighed carefully. Some destinations just require more driving than others, but if we are visiting a city with good public transportation or we are heading to a resort we don't plan to leave for the duration of our visit, a car isn't always necessary. Be sure to weigh the options. Are you mainly concerned with getting to and from the airport? Will the rented car be sitting in a parking lot the rest of the time? Can you walk, take a shuttle, get a taxi, or use public transportation?

On a recent trip to New York City together, we stayed at a hotel near the Newark Airport that offered shuttle service. We were there for three days and needed to get to the transit station every day to head into the city, but the nearest station to the hotel was a two-mile walk each way. Desperately not wanting to rent a car, we did a little more investigating and discovered the airport shuttle would take us between our hotel and the airport as often as we needed—and that the transit system went right to the airport! This discovery saved us the cost of a car rental and a taxi.

HOW TO FIND THE BEST CAR RENTAL RATES

1. Research and compare rates.
   - Note daily and weekly rates and size of the cars. Elisabeth Leamy, consumer correspondent for *Good Morning America*, notes that sometimes a weekly rate will be less than a four- or five-day rental. Get the most for your money! Rental companies group their cars by size but not all of them do it the same way.
   - Look at the details, like proximity to the airport, the hours pick-up and drop-off are available, and if there are any mileage restrictions. Also note that some companies with pick-ups inside the airport charge more than those with pick-ups just outside the airport. (Bonus! Off-airport locations usually offer free shuttles to get their customers to and from the airport and the office.)
2. Look for coupons or online discounts.
   - The Entertainment book is again a good source for coupons. There are always several pages of coupons for travel, including car rentals.
   - Check for package deals before booking air travel. Some of the last-minute getaways include a rental car for considerable savings. The same sites that we recommend for air travel deals will list packages for sale, too.

Saving on a Bed

The spending is just beginning! Deciding where to lay our heads can be a monumental task. Unfortunately, we too often assume our only choice is a national hotel or motel chain. While there are some great deals to be found at these places, other options are worth exploring.

First we'll discuss the pros and cons of hotel and motel chains. There's a big convenience factor here: it's easy to find the amenities we need, including free breakfast (although some definitions of breakfast could use a little work!), and it's easy to book our rooms online. Many hotels offer shuttle services, especially in tourist or downtown areas, and tend to be centralized for vacationers or business travelers or sometimes both. A big drawback for us and other traveling families is that it's harder and harder to find hotels and motels with kitchenettes. Some only have a very small refrigerator and microwave and many have nothing at all. Having a kitchenette is a great, simple way to save our families money on vacation. We also prefer suites so the kids can nap or get to bed on time and we don't have to worry about waking them. However, a suite tends to cost more than a standard room and there is usually a limited number available. Finally, most hotels and motels have laundry machines we can use when staying for an extended time, although they do require quarters, laundry soap, and, usually, a lot of waiting around.

Where to Find a Good Deal on Hotel or Motel Rooms

Hotel prices run the gamut from amazingly good deals to excruciatingly high and everything in between. What makes a good deal on a hotel room depends on what we need it for.

Are we looking for luxury and pampering or a quiet, clean place to catch some sleep before our next adventure? Do we need room service, a kitchenette, a coffeemaker, a pool, laundry facilities, concierge, free Wi-Fi? The list of amenities is endless and the prices vary by city, day, and street corner.

We typically start our search with a travel site like Hotels.com (www.hotels.com), Travelocity, Priceline.com, or Orbitz. These sites nearly always have the lowest rates and the majority of hotels in a given city will be listed. Visit our website for a full listing of travel sites to search.

- We can narrow the results by the amenities we must have and even select a specific part of the city to stay in.
- We make a short list of the hotels that meet our criteria and double-check that we're getting the lowest rates.
- We can do this by visiting the website of the hotel we are considering staying at or even calling the hotel directly to ask what the lowest rate is. There may be additional discounts available on the hotel's own site that are not reflected on a travel site (for example, student, military, senior citizen, or AAA).
- Consider booking business-oriented hotels for a weekend stay or a hotel in a tourist location during the week. You will be more likely to catch the hotel on nights when they are underbooked and willing to make a deal.
- Look into rewards programs.
- When we find a particular hotel chain we like and that is consistently a good value, we may join its rewards program. These programs usually offer a free night after so many stays are completed. Kristin's family has found consistent value in Choice Privileges, a program operated by a company that owns several chains. There are programs for nearly every hotel chain (and airline, too); simply ask at the front desk or visit the company's website.

- Many of the travel sites we've mentioned have their own rewards programs that are worth looking into. Chrissy's family uses Hotels.com, which offers a program that gives her great flexibility to stay at almost any hotel and earn points (as long as she books through the site directly).

Vacation Rentals

Our families both like to get vacation rentals when we go on extended vacations to get that "home away from home" feel. There are obvious benefits to renting a home versus staying at a hotel. Chrissy's family likes to ski in Colorado each year, so they always get together to rent a house where everyone has a room, they can cook and eat family dinners and do laundry, and the kids can play and nap. In general it's a more relaxing environment for their family to "settle in" for a ten-day vacation. Kristin's family likes to visit the beach and always looks for a house or condo to rent because it's more likely to be situated on a private or semiprivate stretch of beach in a quiet community than a hotel would be.

Homes and condos are usually fully furnished and most include dishes and silverware, linens, DVD and CD players, even gaming consoles. It's an even better deal when a group goes together. For example, Chrissy and her husband travel with their extended family each year. On one trip, they rented a million-dollar home with seven bedrooms, five bathrooms, a beautiful kitchen, two living rooms, a game room, and a hot tub for just $70 a night per family. The cheapest hotel room in the area was $100 per night.

Rentals offer more space and often more luxury and added comfort. As a prospective guest, we have the advantage of shopping around and negotiating with rental property owners. They are more likely to come down on their price than a hotel. Of course, there are disadvantages to staying in a home away from home. No one will change the sheets, wash the linens, or clean up the kitchen. Homes also don't offer the same amenities as hotels or condos. There are usually no pools or fitness centers and definitely no room service or vending machines. And while the overall nightly rate may be lower, guests are often required to put down a larger deposit and book well in advance.

> We rented a house on our vacation and loved it! We traveled with family so we all split the cost and only had to pay $50 a night. We had five bedrooms so everyone could spread out and have their own space. It was so nice to have a place the adults could hang out in after the kids went to bed.
>
> —*Nancy*

Tips for Finding a Good Deal and Reserving Vacation Rental Property

Book in advance—we mean months in advance!

- The properties in the best locations and that are the best value will be gobbled up quickly. Usually families are returning year after year so they may book their vacations a full year in advance.
- Chrissy booked her ski-in, ski-out condo nine months in advance because she found a great deal. Her price was 50% less than other condos in the same building. If she had waited even a few weeks, the condo would definitely have been rented to someone else.
- If you can't book in advance, wait until the last minute and try to catch one with a random open weekend or on a cancellation. It's riskier, so you'll need have a backup plan or be willing to move travel dates.

- Find an individual owner instead of renting through an agency or management firm. You're more apt to get a better rate up front or be able to negotiate with them.
- Verify the total amount and understand policies.
- Check on taxes, cleaning fees, administration fees, etc.
- Find out if they will let you clean the property yourself and waive the fee. (If so, what are the cleaning requirements?)

How to Find a Vacation Rental

- Search websites dedicated to vacation rentals, like Vacation Rentals by Owner (www.vrbo.com). Visit our website for a complete, current list of sites.
- Bid on vacation rentals or time-shares on eBay.

All-Inclusive Resorts and Cruises

All-inclusive vacations are a way to take a great vacation for a guaranteed price. Very little planning is required and there are no last-minute surprise expenses; you don't need to budget for meals, hotels, or entertainment. In a vacation package all expenses are included from start to finish. Food, beverages, hotel room or cabin, activities, and events are all part of the up-front costs. Travel to and from your destination or cruise departure point, alcoholic beverages, and souvenirs are typically extra, but not always. All-inclusive vacations do cost more up front but, depending on how good of a deal you get, they may be less expensive than the same trip if you paid for each part separately.

Despite all of the benefits, there are still some disadvantages to consider. For example, while meals are included, there are usually restrictions: you may be limited to visiting a specific restaurant only once during your stay or you might need to make reservations. Chrissy and her husband learned this lesson the hard way. They assumed they didn't need to make restaurant reservations since they were going to an all-inclusive resort. They missed eating at a restaurant they were dying to try because it was already booked up for the week by the time they arrived. Also, watch out if you don't like, say, French cuisine or the local fare, because you may be out of luck. One of Kristin's friends ran into a similar problem at a resort in Mexico where she and her husband honeymooned. They were unhappy with the food available as part of their package and ended up spending an extra $200 to eat at a different restaurant! And it's great that entertainment is included, but watch out if your main reason for taking a cruise to the Bahamas is to go reef diving—some specialty activities and excursions like that cost extra (and by "extra" we mean a lot extra!).

In addition to the restrictions on dining and entertainment, it's important to be prepared to vacation on someone else's schedule. Cruises especially are on a strict departure and arrival schedule. Your cruise may include several ports of call and if you hope to catch a glimpse of these places you have to be on time to take the land excursion and to reboard the ship for departure or risk being left behind. You may also find that reservations are required for dinner at ship restaurants and some shows.

Tips for Finding a Good Deal on All-Inclusive Vacations

Pick the season carefully. Do a little research to find out the high and low seasons for the destination you have chosen. This can equate to several hundred or even a thousand dollars in savings.

Shop around for different deals. You'll find very different prices from resort to resort and between cruise lines.

Be sure to note the services that are included and any specials taxes or fees you'll have to pay (such as port-of-call entry fees or taxes and miscellaneous fees to the resort or cruise line). Taxes and fees alone can be up to $300 per traveler!

Expenses to consider when booking an all-inclusive vacation:

- Drinks (both alcoholic and nonalcoholic)
- Tips and gratuities (some cruise lines and resorts actually won't let you tip while others expect it, so be sure to find out)
- Excursions (land and sea)
- Spa treatments and fitness centers
- Luggage restrictions and charges for going over these limits

Meals and Drinks on a Dime

In addition to all the tips we shared in the previous chapter on entertainment, we have a few specific travel tips to cut the cost of eating on the go!

First, make every attempt to get a room with a kitchenette. A small refrigerator, microwave, and sink will do, but even better would be to have a stove and oven, freezer, and dining table. If we are driving to our destination, we pack as much food as we can get into our vehicle. Use the tips from the earlier chapters on grocery shopping at home (doing this on the road takes a bit more planning) to save a bunch of money! Regardless of how and where you purchase the groceries, eating in will save you 40%–50% on your food while vacationing.

Second, plan a couple of big meals that can serve as leftovers on busy days. Think about things your family loves that are simple to prepare. Meals like spaghetti, tacos, pizza, and breakfast burritos are all easy and make great leftovers. Chrissy's extended family often travels together and rooms in the same house. They save money by purchasing larger quantities of food for planned meals and sharing the cost. Each family has a day when they are responsible for meals, and everyone helps clean up so it's not such a chore.

If only a refrigerator and microwave are available, plan to do easy breakfasts and either lunch or dinner in the room and have a bigger meal at a restaurant, or grab takeout. You will still be saving money on meals but also be able to add a little variety by throwing in a hot meal once a day.

If there is no refrigerator or microwave available or you are spending days in the car or camping, think of foods that don't need refrigeration, like peanut butter and jelly, veggies and hummus, some cheeses, crackers, fruit, and canned meats. These are all easy things to open and eat on the go but they will save a lot of money.

Finally, if you do plan to eat out, be sure to order an Entertainment book for the city you are visiting, in advance of the trip, so you can take advantage of restaurant coupons to save money.

Travel Entertainment and Attractions

Once we arrive at our destination vacation, freedom sets in and we find it hard to say no to attractions and events; that's why we chose that destination, right? To save ourselves from overspending on fun, we do a lot of research on our destination to find out how much activities will cost and how we can save money.

First, know what your budget is, within some reasonable range.

Second, search guidebooks and websites for events and attractions. Travel books from the library are great or head to the book-store with a notebook and spend a couple of hours getting ideas from a current travel guidebook. Websites like Lonely Planet (www.lonelyplanet.com), Real Travel (http://realtravel.com), and Fodor's (www.fodors.com) have great listings of things to do along with links to other websites and references for additional reading. Don't forget to check the city's website for a link to visitor information, or visit the local chamber of commerce site for more city events and links to local businesses. Free activities are often scheduled that are just as fun as the ones you might pay for. Check the local newspaper's website as well, or look for a website made for parents in the city you are visiting. These are surefire ways to read about what's great for families and get some honest reviews. You'll note also that these are the same tricks we use to find out about our local events (from chapter 12). Once you have a list of activities, find out how much they cost and start searching for specials and discounts.

Third, research passes and reciprocity programs. All the same principles from the previous chapter for finding savings on entertainment apply for traveling as well. Plus here are a few extras that might help. Several cities participate in special savings programs like CityPasses (www.citypass.com) and Go City Cards (www.smartdestinations.com). Visitors who buy these cards get paid entrance to several dozen attractions for a predetermined time during the length of their stay. They are typically less expensive per person than buying just one or two individual entrance tickets and are valid for anywhere from three to fourteen days at a time. You may also find great deals that include transportation to and from an attraction (or series of attractions) by visiting TourCorp at www.tourcorp.com. If your family is interested in visiting a museum, science center, or public gardens, be sure to check for free admissions days or take advantage of reciprocity programs you may be eligible for. Reciprocity programs allow members or annual pass holders in one city to enter for free or at a discounted rate within the national network in another city. Association networks are organized by industry (art museums, zoos, gardens and arboretums, etc.) and not every museum is a member of a national organization (but most are).

Check the following sites for more details:

- Zoos and aquariums: www.aza.org/reciprocity/
- Children's museums: www.childrensmuseums.org/visit/reciprocal.htm
- Science and technology centers: www.astc.org/members/passlist.htm
- Art museums: http://sites.google.com/site/northamerican-reciprocalmuseums/north-american-reciprocal-museum-listing
- Botanical gardens, aboretums, and conservatories: www.ahs.org/events/reciprocal_events.htm

It's a good idea to look at your local attractions to see who participates in the reciprocity program most appropriate for you before you buy.

Fourth, be sure to find out what is included in your stay. Some hotels have water parks but admission is only included with certain room types, and sometimes hotels even have organized tours or events that may or may not require reservations and extra fees.

Last but not least, souvenirs! This is especially important for travelers with children. Gift shops are full of cute unique items to help remember your trip by. We suggest discussing your family's souvenir policy with children before setting out on vacation. Many national chain stores will carry some of these same gift shop items for half the price. Consider buying souvenirs at Target, CVS, Walgreens, or Wal-Mart once you arrive at your destination (or even before you leave if possible). Give them to your children at appropriate times during the trip to make it special.

> Before we went to Disney I visited the outlet store and bought several Disney clearance items to bring with us on our trip. Each day of our vacation I gave my children a special "souvenir." I even picked up some Disney T-shirts before we left town. My kids loved getting their souvenirs, they have something special to remember their trip, and I only spent half what the gift shops were asking!
>
> —*Brooke*

Travel Insurance

Travel insurance is nearly always looked at as an unnecessary expense. For big, expensive trips we may be able to justify the expense but we seldom actually make the purchase. Whether we are driving a few hours away or flying cross-country, there are some important things to consider.

Kristin's parents take an annual road trip to Colorado each summer. This trip typically goes without a hitch. However, it only takes one hiccup to remind us that travel insurance can be a huge blessing! On their most recent trip out west, they were driving in the early hours of dawn in western Kansas, an area not known for its abundant population. At around four a.m., they had an accident with a deer. Thankfully, they weren't injured but their vehicle sustained extensive damage. Still several hundred miles from their destination, they were stranded in a town with not much to do, waiting for a mechanic and their auto insurance company to sort out the details. It was a Sunday morning. A rental car would not be covered for the full length of their trip and the last thing they wanted to do was drive to their rented condo only to have to turn around and come back in two days to swap a rental car for their own vehicle. They ended up spending four of their eight vacation days waiting for car repairs, they spent an extra $400 on their hotel, and they were out the cost of the missed nights at their condo (not to mention the insurance deductible resulting from the accident). If they'd had travel insurance, the cost of any missed travel plans would have been covered as well as the additional hotel room and maybe even a tow to the repair shop.

Some travel insurance is included with certain memberships, credit cards, and packages, but other insurance must be purchased separately. It can seem costly but consider where you might be during your travels and what things may go wrong along the way. Would you be able to cover the costs? Would your vacation plans (and associated costs) be out the window? If so, it might be prudent to purchase insurance. Also, make sure to check your current insurance to see what it covers before you leave. On Chrissy's honeymoon in Hawaii, her husband lost his wedding band in the ocean two days after their arrival. Worried that this same fate would befall Chrissy, she slipped her ring off and left it in her wallet in their rental car the next time they went to the beach. Unfortunately, their vehicle was broken into while they were at the beach that day and her wallet, with the ring inside, was taken (you can't make up stories like these!). Thankfully, they had been careful to insure their rings on their homeowner's policy and everything else was covered under their car insurance.

Centsable Tips for Traveling with Kids

Traveling with small children adds a whole new set of what-ifs to the vacation scenario. We've discovered that taking time to do some things differently will save money and create a more relaxed environment.

> We planned the perfect vacation our family had been dreaming about all year! We did everything right, except we got lost in the fun and skipped our kids' naps and let them stay up late. By the third day of vacation we had complete anarchy! It took two days and an enormous amount of patience to get things back to manageable and we wasted so much time! If we had stopped the first two days to make sure they were rested and in bed on time we would have enjoyed days three, four, and five much more and been able to save money doing the things we had spent time planning rather than spending money on snacks, missed events, and random activities to appease two very distraught toddlers!
>
> —*Lisa*

Respect Their Schedules!

Young children may seem so full of excitement and anticipation that they don't need downtime, but as the parents we must remember that they cannot anticipate what will happen next. They don't realize that staying up late and skipping a nap means they will be out of control the next day. Build space into your vacation schedule for downtime. Return to your hotel room or rental unit for lunch and a movie or nap, call it a day in time to catch dinner before the kids are starving, and make it back in time for a bath and bed or a book. Whatever the ritual is at home, try to follow it on vacation.

Plan activities that the whole family will enjoy, but be strategic about it. If a sit-down show or other quiet activity is on the agenda, make sure you get to enjoy it by planning it for early in the day or giving children a chance to be active beforehand so they are ready to sit.

Plan meals at the appropriate mealtimes and always have snacks and drinks on hand just in case!

When flying, prepare children for the process of security checks and boarding the plane. Talk to them about the sights and sounds and who they might meet. Again, have snacks and some activities for them to stay occupied. Books, small puzzles, cards, and pocket-size paper and crayons are perfect.

If you are driving a long distance, plan for frequent stops for little ones to stretch their legs and take a break. They are stuck in a car seat with no concept of how much time has passed or how much is left. This makes for a disgruntled passenger if ever there was one! Consider driving mostly at nap time and bedtime if your children aren't agreeable travelers. Chrissy's family usually drives during the night hours so their two children can sleep on the way.

Be sure to pack lots of food and plan to stop for picnics along the way. Even if the weather's not good you can find an indoor visitor's center to stop and eat in. Be sure that you pack healthy foods. Riding in a car for several hours at a time can cause small children to become uncomfortable or have an upset stomach. Adding sugary, fatty foods to that may make it worse and ruin your trip altogether! Also consider the quantity and type of beverages you are providing for small children. Things like juice and flavored waters and drinks may result in many, many more bathroom stops and diaper changes than anticipated. Speaking of bathroom breaks, we always take our potty chairs with us on road trips. When our four-year-olds say they have to go to the restroom, they usually mean right now, not in ten minutes when we will pass a McDonald's or rest stop. A potty chair helps ensure that we don't have to strip the car seat of its padding to wash it! We have made dozens of stops on the side of the road to use the potty chair and every time we remembered why we brought it and gave it a special spot right up front by the car seats.

If and when you decide to stop for meals, consider places that the kids can run around in or play or get some time to just relax. Kid-friendly restaurants with a variety of food choices are best. Buffets, mall food courts, restaurants like Chick-fil-A, and stores like IKEA that have a play area and healthier menu options are all good choices.

Of all the road trip preparations we've discussed with other parents, none have elicited as much commentary and opinion as the use of a DVD player. While we yearn for our kids to enjoy the scenery and the beauty of cross-country road trips, when boredom sets in and we've decided we are not stopping the car one more time until we reach our destination, the DVD player has been our only saving grace!

With these tips you can sit back and enjoy your vacation and make lasting family memories on a budget.

Action Plan

1. When planning your next trip, find the answer to these questions:
   a. What are the high and low seasons for the destination?
   b. Should we book early or wait until the last minute?
2. Check out BeCentsable.net for:
   a. Links to great travel and activity sites.
   b. Road and air travel survival guides for families.

Conclusion

A s we look back on our journey thus far, we are struck by how many things have remained the same while we have dramatically changed our actions and approach. We don't have less now and we aren't sacrificing quality. On the contrary, we buy higher-quality products now than we used to! We were both intelligent, resourceful women of modest means, and typically we were prudent with our resources (at least, we can say we were never extravagant!). So how could we have literally been throwing money away? We realize now the answer is simple and applies equally to every other family like ours. It was not a lack of desire or a tendency toward wastefulness; it was lack of knowledge.

We often regarded saving money as a time-consuming effort we literally could not engage in. Throughout this book we hope it's been clear that any time we now spend saving money replaces time we would have spent either in the store trying to organize our thoughts or at home trying to use the things we purchased. We look at our methods and planning as earning money rather than saving it. We find that having a dinner plan each week, for example, means we can spend more time visiting with friends, playing with our children, or simply relaxing. Having a plan that also saves money means we have room for more fun in our lives!

As we came to realize the impact these things were having on our overall lives, we knew we needed to share the information. We knew families of all means could truly and deeply benefit from these skills. As active members of our local moms' club, we were friends with several mothers who were working part-time jobs to help with the family's finances, to meet specific obligations, or just to add to the vacation budget. What empowerment our friends would feel when they could save the same amount of money each week that they were leaving their families to earn!

In the process of talking about our program and teaching our friends, we felt the need for a clear, reliable, complete, and concise resource—a one-stop guide to saving every day. We thought through the many ways we could communicate to those who, like us, simply did not have the knowledge. The challenge was not a lack of information; on the contrary, there was too much information in far too many places. We needed to narrow the touch points. The people, websites, blogs, and forums that had been our references in the learning process became our inspiration.

Creating a BeCentsable Program

In January 2008, BeCentsable was born. At first we created a simple written guide for those who wanted to learn what they could do and how. A month later we invited our moms' club friends into Chrissy's living room and held our first workshop.

Since the beginning, we have felt the most important step

shoppers can take to save money is to *learn*. As word spread about our workshops and our blog continued to grow and evolve, demand increased more quickly than our availability.

Our workshops were initially only presented live in someone's home (that continues to be the primary and most useful format). In these workshops we put an emphasis not only on teaching strategies but on changing the way our "students" think about shopping. The BeCentsable program is a *money-earning* activity rather than a money-saving one. For many families, this education can provide more "wiggle room" in their budget than a part-time job.

In-person workshops are encouraging and inspirational. Attendees are usually friends or family and they have similar shopping experiences. Having many individuals' experiences to connect with and draw on also fosters community, something at the heart of our program. Community makes it possible. We would not be able to offer the help and guidance we do without the constant support of other women and men across the country who blog, publish websites, and share their experiences with us each day.

By the spring of 2008, we had laid the foundation for our blog to be a nationwide resource for families just like ours. By that summer, we had developed a program to train people across the country how to teach our workshops in their own communities. Just one year after beginning our mission, the BeCentsable Educator program was launched. Just one short month later we were surprised to be featured on *Good Morning America*. After our *Good Morning America* story aired, we found ourselves in a happy (albeit unexpected) position. The sudden media interest fueled by a national desire to cut back on spending turned our living room meeting into a nationwide event! For two moms who had never so much as been on local television, this was exciting, exhausting, and definitely a learning experience.

We expanded our BeCentsable Educator program across the

country and were thrilled to be helping so many people save money, time, and resources. We have received e-mails every week with thanks for how much the BeCentsable program has helped families across the country. Some of these families are struggling with the same financial pressures many have had to face in recent years: serious illness or a death in the family, bankruptcy, and near homelessness. Others are thankfully financially stable and looking for ways to secure their future through increased savings. Either way, our program offers them concrete steps to take and the knowledge to move forward quickly.

Our website, workshops, and book all serve to fulfill our heartfelt mission:

> To help families save money, time, and resources so they can focus on more important things; and to offer the tools and encouragement to help them spread the wealth, using their new skills to improve their communities.

As we reflect how quickly BeCentsable has grown in such a short time, we know in our hearts that it is to help fulfill this mission. We encourage everyone to use the strategies we teach in our book, on our website, and in our workshops toward the greater good. Not all of us can give a great deal of time or money, maybe none at all. But we can take full advantage of opportunities that are presented to us. A free or nearly free can of food one week at the grocery store saves a family or food bank from spending money to buy it.

We often wonder what might happen if each family was able to give just one item a week using the skills we teach.

By taking advantage of simple deals at local shops, Kristin was able to put together a handful of baskets for her local women's shelter and donated $160 worth of groceries for just $26. The ladies at the shelter received $40 gift baskets full of lotions, teas, soaps, picture frames, and miscellaneous stationery as Christmas gifts, and Kristin only paid about $7 to fill them.

Even if you can't give money, food, or gifts, consider sharing your knowledge. Educate friends and family (even new acquaintances) about how you are saving. You will be giving them the gift of time and money, providing others with additional resources to make life more meaningful for their families by whatever means that may be.

It truly has been an amusing, enlightening, and insightful journey for us as friends and for our families. We have come a long way since we started this adventure and are excited to continue sharing what we've learned.

Index

Note: Page numbers followed by a *t* refer to text boxes